UNDERSTANDING SCIENCE & NATURE

Plant Life

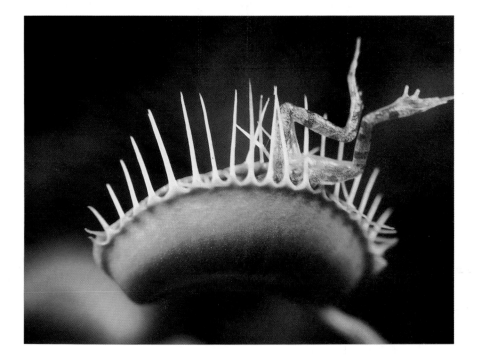

TIME-LIFE
ALEXANDRIA, VIRGINIA

CONTENTS

6 Plants without Flowers

7 Astonishing Adapters

8 The Human Connection

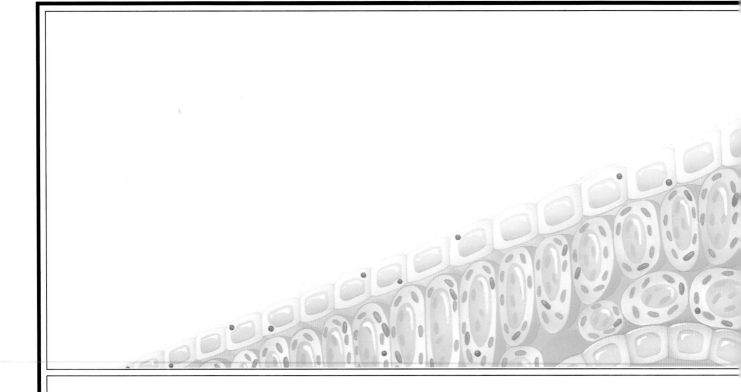

1
Plant Cells
and Growth

Every living being is made of cells. A single cell is all there is to a simple organism, such as a bacterium or an alga, while higher plants and animals may be made of trillions of cells. An oak, for example, has root cells that absorb water and minerals from the soil; leaf cells that produce sugar from sunlight, carbon dioxide, and water; rigid cells in its trunk that support the giant tree; and dozens of other types of cells, each with a specific function.

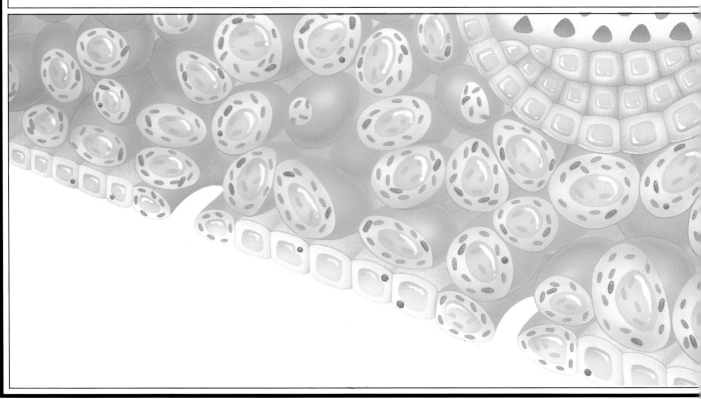

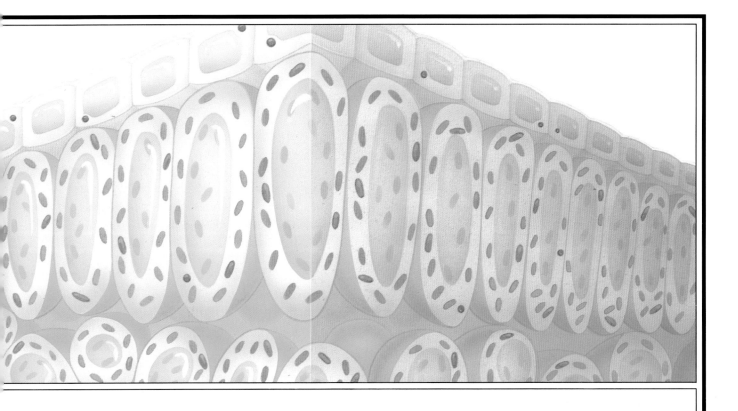

A cell is a mass of water, nutrients, and other chemicals surrounded by a membrane. Plant and animal cells also contain many small structures, called organelles, that carry out certain activities. Photosynthesis, the sun-powered process by which plants make sugar, occurs in organelles called chloroplasts. Mitochondria, another type of organelle, convert the sugar into energy that the cell uses to stay in good working order. With enough energy, a cell will grow and divide into two new cells, each with its own organelles. As the number of cells increases, the organism itself grows larger.

An enlarged cross section of a leaf shows some of the different types of plant cells. Each cell has a nucleus, containing genetic information, and dozens of chloroplasts, which house the cell's food-producing machinery. A cavity called a vacuole stores food and other nutrients, such as minerals

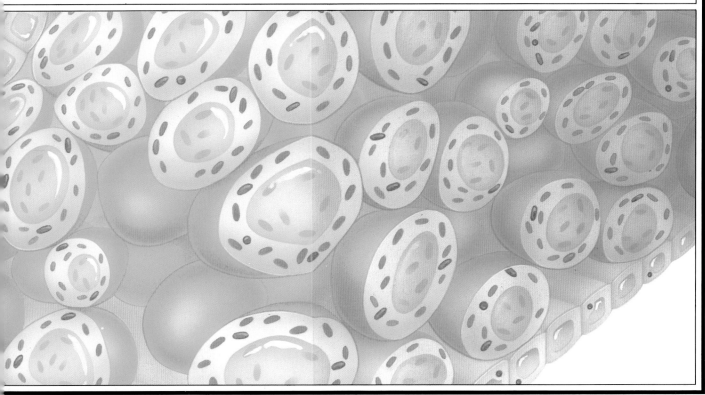

What Is inside a Plant Cell?

Cells are active living units resembling tiny chemical factories. In order to grow, cells must continually manufacture proteins, fats, sugars, and other molecules that make up the cell's membrane, organelles, and various other components. To keep going, cells have to produce energy. Animal cells get energy from the food the animal eats, whereas plants use photosynthesis to manufacture their own food from carbon dioxide and water.

Many of a cell's chemical activities occur in its organelles. The mitochondria are the cell's power plants, converting sugars into energy. Ribosomes, beadlike structures that cover the endoplasmic reticulum—the system of interconnected membranes that functions in transporting material in a cell—produce the cell's proteins. The cell nucleus contains one or more nucleoli, which manufacture ribosomes, and the chromosomes. These hold the genetic information that tells the ribosomes which proteins to make. The Golgi body stores various substances that the cell later channels to other cells.

Chloroplasts are organelles found only in plant cells. They contain chlorophyll, a green pigment, and other molecules that perform photosynthesis. This process uses the energy in sunlight to make sugar from carbon dioxide and water. A plant cell uses some of this sugar itself and stores the rest as starch. When an animal eats a plant, it turns this starch back into sugars, which the mitochondria in its cells use to make energy.

Cell organelles

All animal and plant cells

The nucleus contains a cell's genes and one or more nucleoli.

The endoplasmic reticulum is dotted with ribosomes, which make proteins.

The Golgi body stores substances made in the endoplasmic reticulum.

Mitochondria are a cell's energy factories. A thick membrane surrounds them.

Plant cells only

A strong cell wall, made of the carbohydrate cellulose, encloses the cell membrane.

Photosynthesis occurs in chloroplasts, which contain the pigment chlorophyll.

Vacuoles contain sap. They are surrounded by a membrane called the tonoplast.

Animal cells only

Centrosomes are bundles of fibers. More fibers sprout when a cell divides.

Golgi body

Nucleus — Nuclear membrane
Genetic material (DNA)
Nucleolus

Centrosome

Mitochondria

Endoplasmic reticulum

Ribosome

Cell membrane

Mitochondria

Golgi body

Animal cell

Typical cells

Organelles take up most of the space inside plant cells *(below, right)* and animal cells *(below, left)*. A fluid, cytoplasm, surrounds the organelles.

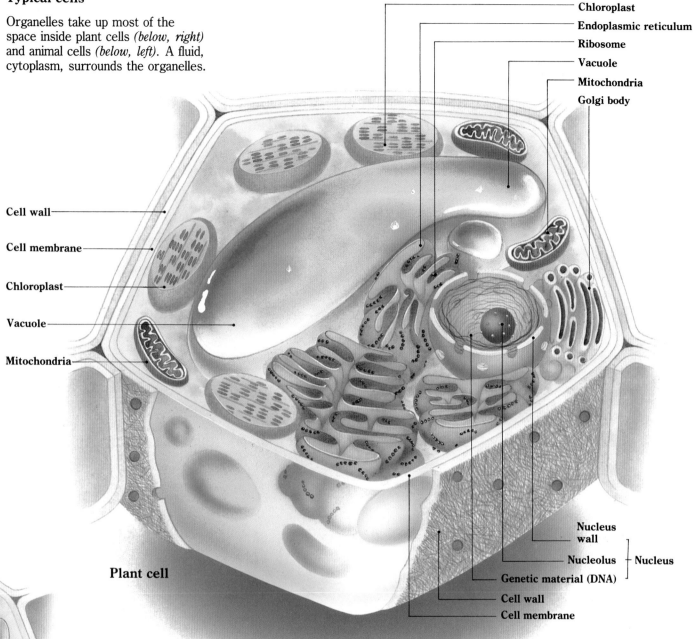

Plant cell

Cell wall
Cell membrane
Chloroplast
Vacuole
Mitochondria

Chloroplast
Endoplasmic reticulum
Ribosome
Vacuole
Mitochondria
Golgi body

Nucleus wall
Nucleolus — Nucleus
Genetic material (DNA)
Cell wall
Cell membrane

Inside plant and animal cells

Typically, both plant and animal cells have a nucleus and a number of organelles such as mitochondria, the Golgi body, and the endoplasmic reticulum. These structures float in a liquid called cytoplasm and are surrounded by the cell membrane. Plant cells also have a sturdy cell wall made of cellulose. Two types of organelles—chloroplasts and a vacuole—are unique to plant cells. Photosynthesis occurs in chloroplasts, which appear green because they contain the pigment chlorophyll. Young plant cells contain several small vacuoles that grow and eventually merge as the cell matures. Plant cells lack the pair of centrosomes found in animal cells. Centrosomes play a role in animal-cell division.

Storage grains

Plant cells store excess nutrients and waste products in tiny grains visible only under a microscope. Fructose, for example, is stored in inulin grains.

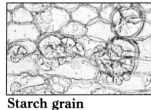

Starch grain

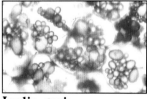

Inulin grain

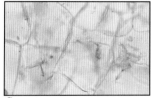

Carotene

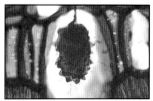

Calcium carbonate

How Does a Plant Make Seeds?

Most of the plants alive today belong to two large classes, the gymnosperms and the angiosperms. These two classes are the higher plants that produce seeds from fertilized ovules, which consist of embryonic sacs and their protective tissues. Gymnosperms, which include fir, spruce, hemlock, pine, larch, and ginkgo trees, produce "naked seeds"—seeds that are not surrounded by an ovary. Most are produced inside cones, though juniper and yew seeds are covered with flesh resembling that of a berry. Angiosperms, or flowering plants, occur in an almost endless variety and include nearly all the world's crops. All flowering plants produce seeds within an ovary, or fruit, as shown here. Apples and oranges are fruits; but so, too, are cucumbers and corn.

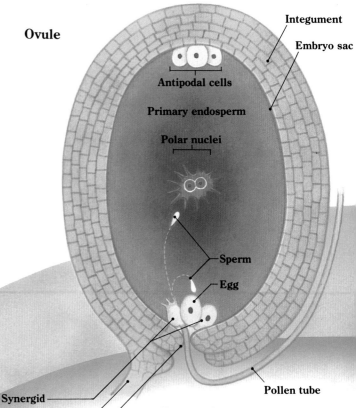

Ovule

Integument

Embryo sac

Antipodal cells

Primary endosperm

Polar nuclei

Sperm

Egg

Pollen tube

Synergid

Funicle, or stalk of ovule sac

Micropyle

Cross section of a shepherd's-purse flower

Double fertilization

A pollen grain pushes its pollen tube through the micropyle, a small opening in the integument that covers the ovule. Sperm emerge from the pollen tube. One sperm fertilizes the egg. A second sperm fertilizes the polar nuclei within the endosperm mother cell.

Rosette   Germination   Dormant seeds

The resulting fruit cracks open from the bottom and drops its seeds on the ground. The seeds germinate in autumn, producing first a root and then a rosette of leaves.

The shepherd's-purse, a relative of the wild mustard, is a common garden weed. It has white flowers, which grow from a central stem. Butterflies carry the pollen from flower to flower.

Encased in the protective and nutritive tissue of the ovule, the fertilized egg grows rapidly at first.

The egg begins to divide, forming a protoembryo. A cell membrane develops along the walls of the endosperm nucleus.

A germ cell develops at the tip of the protoembryo. At the other end, a cell anchors the embryo into the parental tissue.

The growing line of cells, known as the suspensor, pushes the embryo into the endosperm. The suspensor also serves to carry nutrients to the embryo.

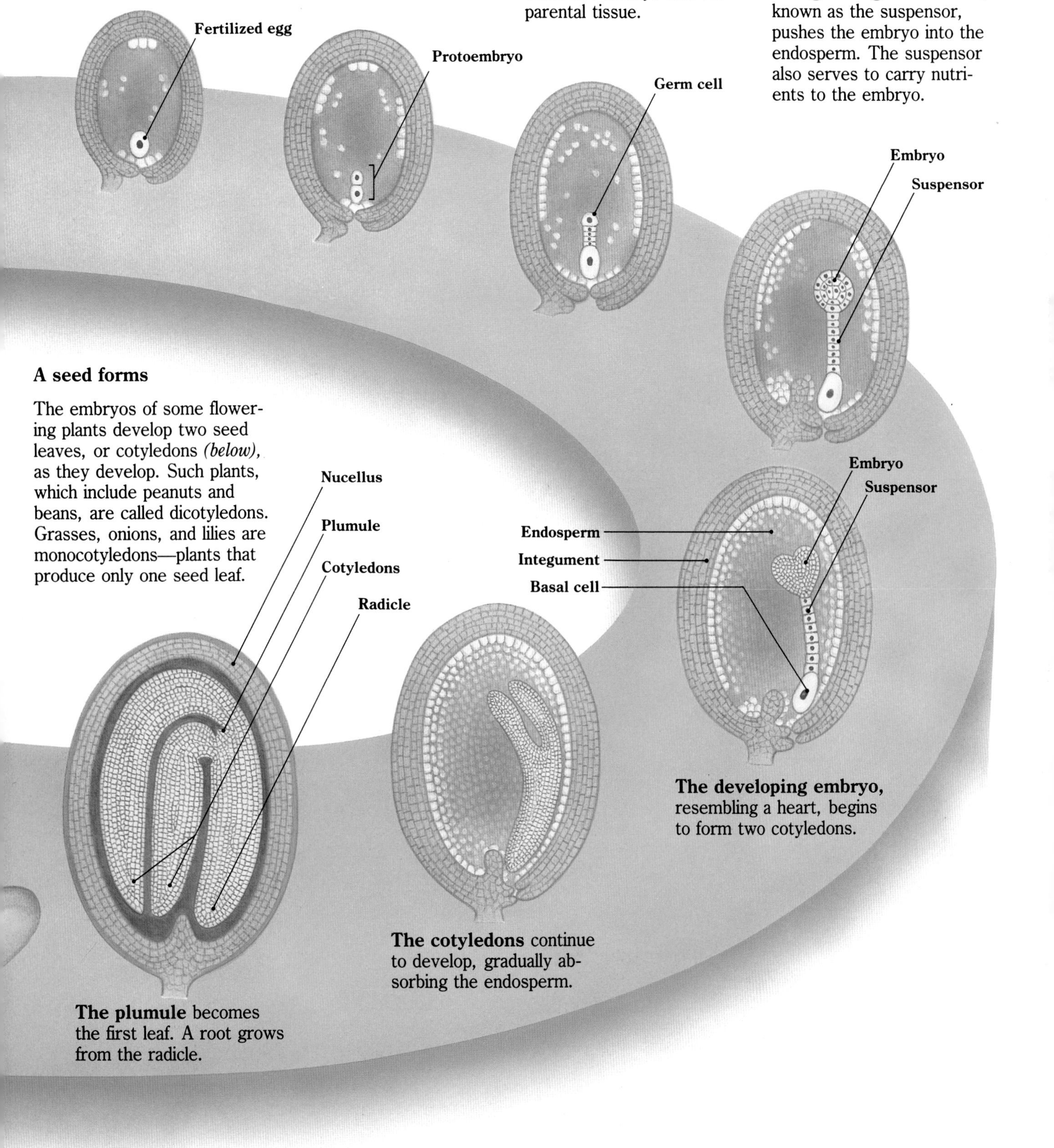

Fertilized egg

Protoembryo

Germ cell

Embryo

Suspensor

A seed forms

The embryos of some flowering plants develop two seed leaves, or cotyledons *(below),* as they develop. Such plants, which include peanuts and beans, are called dicotyledons. Grasses, onions, and lilies are monocotyledons—plants that produce only one seed leaf.

Nucellus

Plumule

Cotyledons

Radicle

Embryo

Suspensor

Endosperm

Integument

Basal cell

The developing embryo, resembling a heart, begins to form two cotyledons.

The cotyledons continue to develop, gradually absorbing the endosperm.

The plumule becomes the first leaf. A root grows from the radicle.

How Do Plants Use Sunlight?

Animals must constantly search for food, but plants just stand still and make their own food. They use the energy in sunlight to convert carbon dioxide and water drawn from air and soil into sugar. This process, called photosynthesis, occurs within a plant's leaves. Carbon dioxide enters a leaf through tiny pores, called stomas, whereas water is transported to the leaves from the roots. The by-product of photosynthesis is the oxygen released by plants, which animals must breathe to live.

Photosynthesis provides a plant with all the food energy it needs to grow. Plants, however, also require other nutrients, such as phosphorus, nitrogen, potassium, and iron, to remain healthy. Plants obtain these substances from the soil through their roots.

Structure of a chloroplast

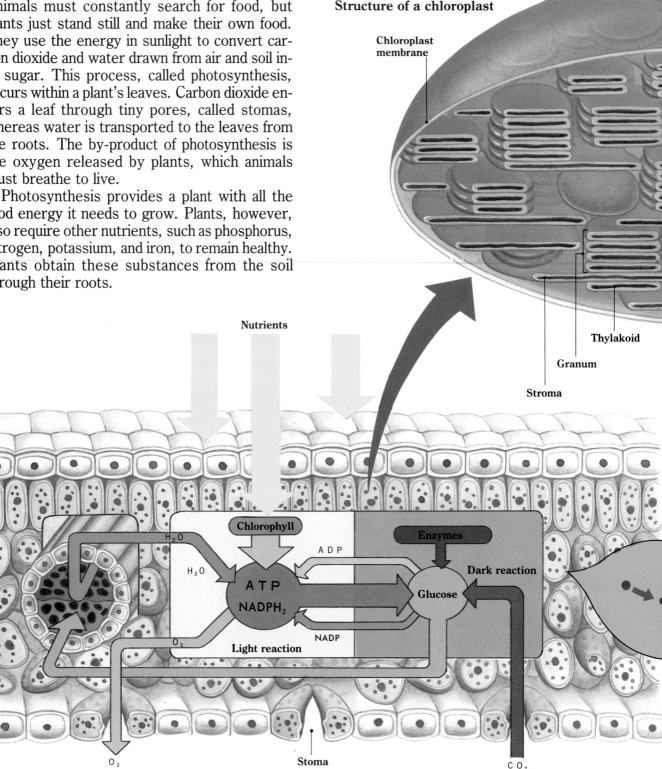

Photosynthesis

Photosynthesis occurs in two sets of chemical reactions, which occur in sequence. In the first set, known as the light-dependent reactions, chlorophyll and other pigments absorb sunlight and use that solar energy to produce the energy-transferring molecules adenosine triphosphate (ATP) and nicotinamide adenine dinucle-otide phosphate, coenzyme II (NADPH$_2$). These chemical reactions consume water (H$_2$O) and release oxygen (O$_2$). In the second set, the so-called dark or light-independent reactions, enzymes use the energy stored in ATP and NADPH$_2$ to combine carbon dioxide (CO$_2$) with water, producing sugars.

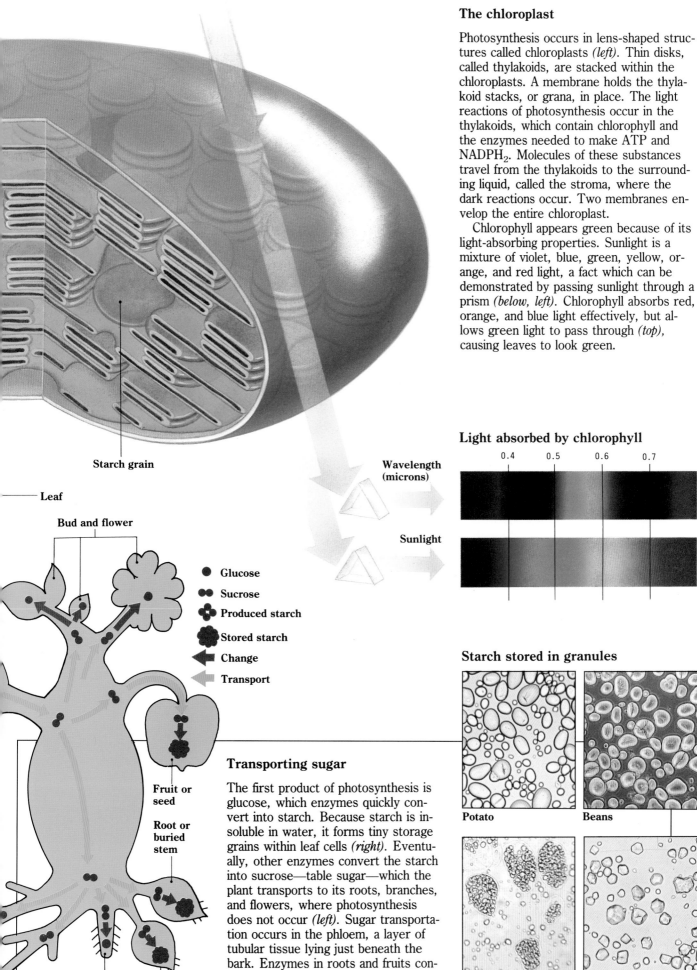

The chloroplast

Photosynthesis occurs in lens-shaped structures called chloroplasts *(left)*. Thin disks, called thylakoids, are stacked within the chloroplasts. A membrane holds the thylakoid stacks, or grana, in place. The light reactions of photosynthesis occur in the thylakoids, which contain chlorophyll and the enzymes needed to make ATP and $NADPH_2$. Molecules of these substances travel from the thylakoids to the surrounding liquid, called the stroma, where the dark reactions occur. Two membranes envelop the entire chloroplast.

Chlorophyll appears green because of its light-absorbing properties. Sunlight is a mixture of violet, blue, green, yellow, orange, and red light, a fact which can be demonstrated by passing sunlight through a prism *(below, left)*. Chlorophyll absorbs red, orange, and blue light effectively, but allows green light to pass through *(top)*, causing leaves to look green.

Starch grain

Leaf

Bud and flower

● **Glucose**

●● **Sucrose**

✦ **Produced starch**

Stored starch

◀ **Change**

◀ **Transport**

Light absorbed by chlorophyll

0.4   0.5   0.6   0.7

Wavelength (microns)

Sunlight

Starch stored in granules

Fruit or seed

Root or buried stem

Transporting sugar

The first product of photosynthesis is glucose, which enzymes quickly convert into starch. Because starch is insoluble in water, it forms tiny storage grains within leaf cells *(right)*. Eventually, other enzymes convert the starch into sucrose—table sugar—which the plant transports to its roots, branches, and flowers, where photosynthesis does not occur *(left)*. Sugar transportation occurs in the phloem, a layer of tubular tissue lying just beneath the bark. Enzymes in roots and fruits convert sucrose into starch for storage.

Young root

Potato

Beans

Pumpkin

Corn

What Causes Seeds to Sprout?

Some seeds will germinate soon after they form, but most seeds must become dormant to mature. Dormant seeds can remain inactive for years or even centuries before germinating. In one case, Oriental lotus seeds recovered from peat bogs near Tokyo germinated after lying dormant for more than 1,000 years.

Seeds will germinate when they receive enough water and oxygen to support the biochemical reactions of life. Dormant seeds are dry, containing less than 10 percent water, and the organelles and other cellular components are virtually invisible under a microscope. But as soon as a dormant seed absorbs water from the soil, it swells rapidly, giving the cells of the seed a chance to expand to normal size. The mitochondria organelles begin taking in oxygen and producing energy from the stored starch, and the embryo within the seed begins to grow. Soon, if the conditions are good, a tiny root appears, absorbing more water and other nutrients from the soil. Suddenly, one day the seed pops out of the ground, lifted skyward by a growing stem. Before long leaves sprout, and the small seedling is on its way to becoming a mature plant.

A seed germinates

A bean seed germinates *(below)* when the radicle, or embryonic root, absorbs water from the soil and bursts through the seed coat. The radicle starts pushing down into the soil and soon grows into branching roots. Meanwhile, the hypocotyl, the stem arising from the embryo, forces its way up through the soil, carrying the seed coat and seed leaves with it. The seed leaves emerge from the seed coat, followed by the first leaves. The seed leaves then wither and fall off.

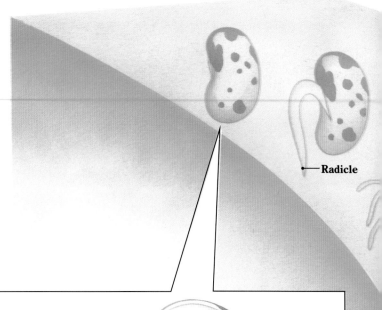

Radicle

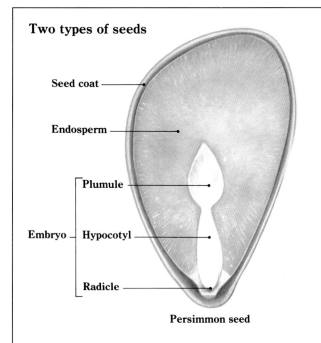

Two types of seeds

Seed coat

Endosperm

Plumule

Embryo — Hypocotyl

Radicle

Persimmon seed

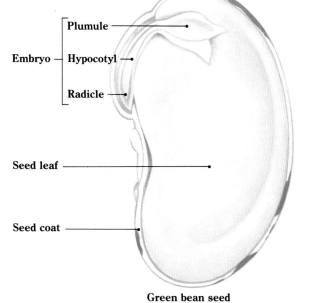

Embryo — Plumule

Hypocotyl

Radicle

Seed leaf

Seed coat

Green bean seed

Plants use two different systems to store food to nourish a germinating seed. Persimmon *(above, left)* and corn, for example, store nutrients in the endosperm, which occupies much of the inside of the seed. The endosperm contains starch, fats, and proteins. Other seeds, such as those of the green bean *(above, right)* and orchid, have almost no endosperm.

Instead, they possess two large seed leaves. As the seed matures on the plant, the seed leaves grow and absorb most of the food stored in the endosperm. In some plants, such as the sunflower, the seed leaves will pop above ground when the seed germinates and begins its photosynthesis, which provides extra nutrition for the newly sprouted plant.

Conditions for germination

Seeds require water, oxygen, and warm temperatures to germinate. Without water, a seed is little more than a package of dehydrated enzymes and organelles. Once a seed becomes wet, it rapidly swells into action. If temperatures are high enough to warm the soil, the seed will use oxygen from the soil to burn stored sugar and begin to grow.

For some seeds, though, water, oxygen, and warmth are not enough to spark germination. Certain grass and lettuce seeds, for example, require light to begin germinating, whereas other seeds will not germinate unless they are in darkness. The seeds of some ash trees need to be frozen to germinate; seeds of the lodgepole pine will not germinate unless they have been heated in a fire.

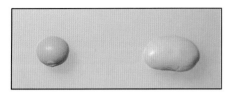

A dry soybean *(left)*; one that has absorbed water *(right)*.

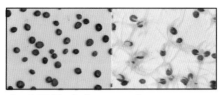

At 86° F., balsam seeds sprout in four days *(right)*.

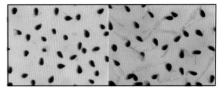

Some seeds, such as onion seeds, germinate best in the dark *(right)*.

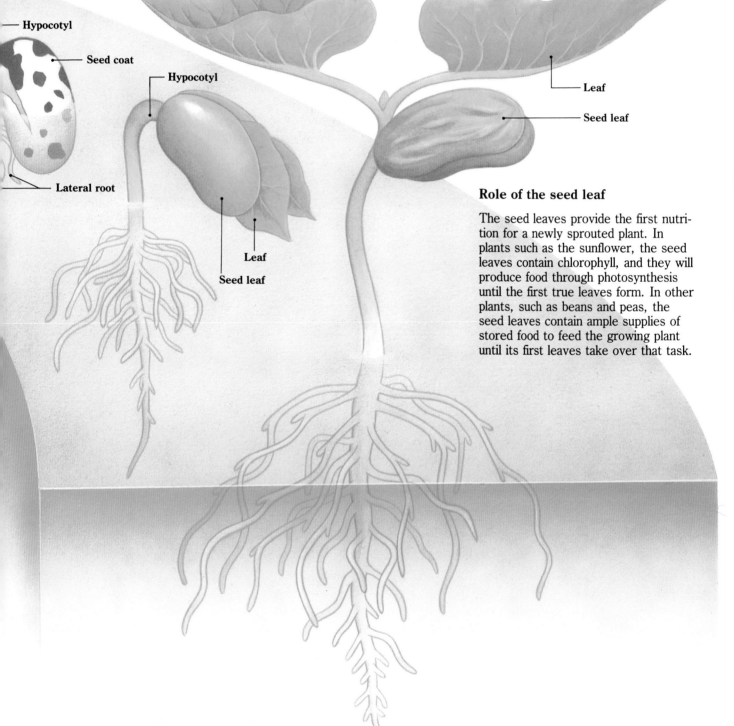

- Hypocotyl
- Seed coat
- Lateral root
- Hypocotyl
- Leaf
- Seed leaf
- Leaf
- Seed leaf

Role of the seed leaf

The seed leaves provide the first nutrition for a newly sprouted plant. In plants such as the sunflower, the seed leaves contain chlorophyll, and they will produce food through photosynthesis until the first true leaves form. In other plants, such as beans and peas, the seed leaves contain ample supplies of stored food to feed the growing plant until its first leaves take over that task.

How Do Roots Grow?

From the moment a seed germinates, its newly emerged root begins forcing its way down into the soil in search of water and various nutrients such as phosphorus and nitrogen. Cells at the root's tip, called the ground meristem, grow and divide at a rapid clip. A thimble-shaped cap protects the dividing cells and smooths the root's passage through the soil. The outer layer of the cap is constantly damaged as it rubs against soil particles, but it is renewed by the rapidly growing meristem. Cells near the edge of the cap and meristem secrete chemicals that keep the root growing downward.

A root's main function is to absorb water from the surrounding soil. To accomplish this, mature sections of root sprout tiny hairs that force their way between individual, water-coated soil particles. Large secondary roots also branch off the main root to provide additional water-absorbing capacity. These lateral roots grow from the central portion of the main root instead of from the root tip and form a small wound in the root when they first break through the root's external layer. This wound, if not sealed quickly, can provide a place for harmful bacteria and viruses to infect the plant.

A root grows

A newly emerged root *(below, left)* is marked with ink bands in an experiment to demonstrate where growth occurs. Cells at the tip grow rapidly, forcing the tip down into the soil and away from the bands *(below, right)*. The distance between the ink bands does not increase, indicating that this part of the root is not growing.

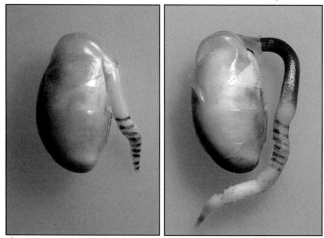

A new root grows fastest at its tip.

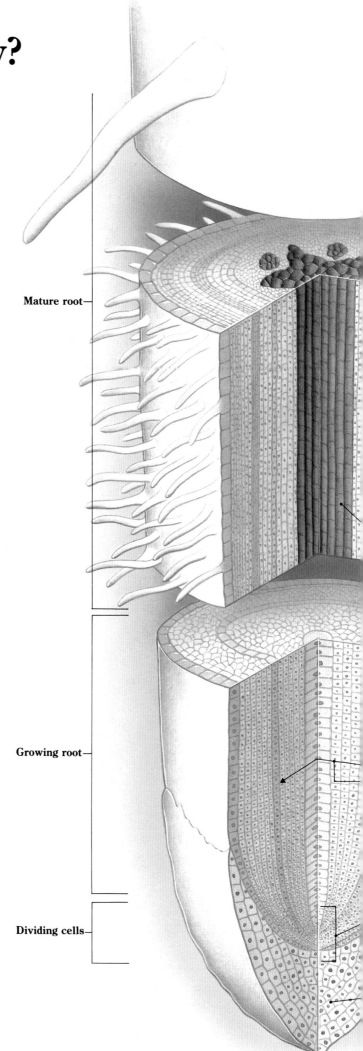

Mature root—

Growing root—

Dividing cells—

The structure of a root

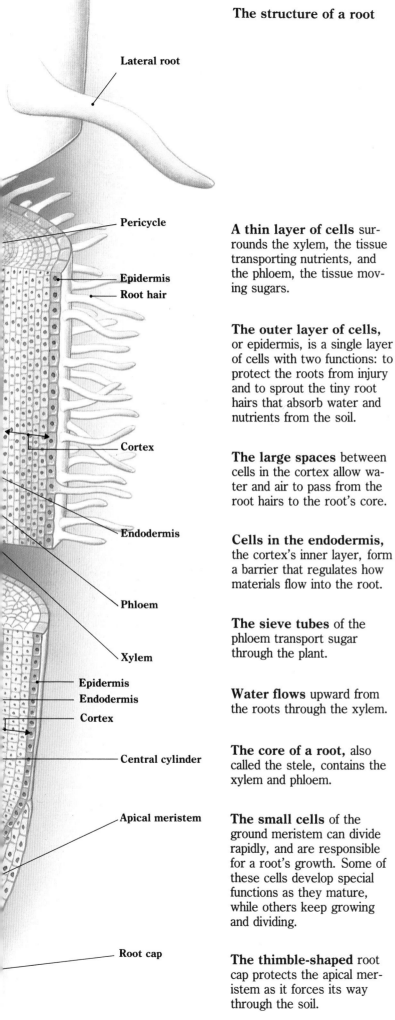

Lateral root

Pericycle

Epidermis
Root hair

Cortex

Endodermis

Phloem

Xylem

Epidermis
Endodermis
Cortex

Central cylinder

Apical meristem

Root cap

A thin layer of cells surrounds the xylem, the tissue transporting nutrients, and the phloem, the tissue moving sugars.

The outer layer of cells, or epidermis, is a single layer of cells with two functions: to protect the roots from injury and to sprout the tiny root hairs that absorb water and nutrients from the soil.

The large spaces between cells in the cortex allow water and air to pass from the root hairs to the root's core.

Cells in the endodermis, the cortex's inner layer, form a barrier that regulates how materials flow into the root.

The sieve tubes of the phloem transport sugar through the plant.

Water flows upward from the roots through the xylem.

The core of a root, also called the stele, contains the xylem and phloem.

The small cells of the ground meristem can divide rapidly, and are responsible for a root's growth. Some of these cells develop special functions as they mature, while others keep growing and dividing.

The thimble-shaped root cap protects the apical meristem as it forces its way through the soil.

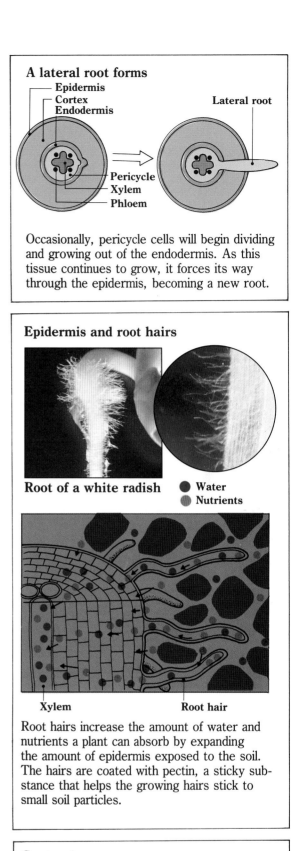

A lateral root forms

Epidermis
Cortex
Endodermis

Lateral root

Pericycle
Xylem
Phloem

Occasionally, pericycle cells will begin dividing and growing out of the endodermis. As this tissue continues to grow, it forces its way through the epidermis, becoming a new root.

Epidermis and root hairs

Root of a white radish

● Water
● Nutrients

Xylem   Root hair

Root hairs increase the amount of water and nutrients a plant can absorb by expanding the amount of epidermis exposed to the soil. The hairs are coated with pectin, a sticky substance that helps the growing hairs stick to small soil particles.

Geotropism

A root placed sideways (*above, left*) will soon react to gravity by growing downward—a response called positive geotropism. Special cells respond to gravity by secreting auxin, a chemical that affects the cells' growth rate.

What Makes Stems and Leaves Grow?

When a plant first emerges from the ground, a single shoot, perhaps with one or two juvenile leaves, begins growing toward the sun. The shoot grows taller at its tip and wider at its base, and all the while new leaves sprout from the growing stem. A little nodule—a bud—soon appears on the stem, and suddenly the bud becomes a new stem branching off from the first one. Now there are two stems sprouting leaves; then more buds appear, and more stems. From a tiny seed a mighty oak is growing.

At the same time that a stem is growing longer at its tip, the inside of the new stem is also changing. Cells grow larger and take on specific roles.

A growing shoot

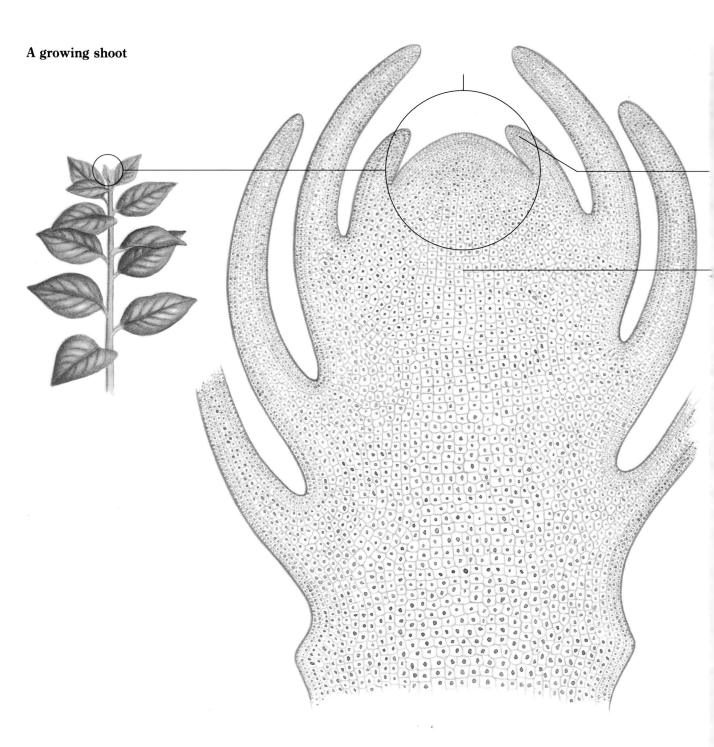

Some cells, for example, die, become hollow, and form the xylem, the tissue that transports water from the roots to the rest of the plant. Others produce a coat of lignin, a stiff material that gives the stem its strength. There are changes, too, within the leaf. The outer layer of cells, called the epidermis, develops a protective coating that keeps the leaf from losing water. Other cells on the surface guard the pores that admit carbon dioxide and allow oxygen to escape. Most cells beneath the surface produce chlorophyll and carry out photosynthesis. The remaining cells form the veins that transport food from the leaves to the rest of the plant.

The apical meristem, or shoot apex, is the place where new stems and leaves form. Cells divide and grow rapidly here. Special cells in a stem's tip produce the chemical auxin, a growth stimulator, which softens the cell wall and allows the stem to continue growing.

Buds form where the growing point and the stem meet. Rudimentary leaves appear on either side of the shoot apex, developing in opposite, alternate, or whorled patterns of leaves.

The ground meristem produces several different types of cells. One type gives the stem its strength; another provides flexibility, allowing the plant to bend without breaking. A third type stores water and food.

Growth of a leaf

Leaves grow in one of the two ways shown above and in the experiment below, in which leaves have been marked with a grid. Leaves of grain plants, such as the corn plant here, grow only at the base of the leaf. The markings move up as the leaf grows.

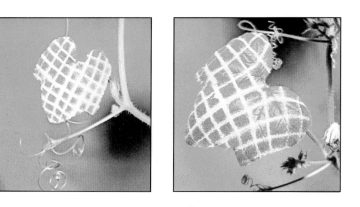

Growth of leaves and stems

In broad-leaved plants, such as the sponge gourd at left, all cells in the leaf's blade grow and divide. The experiment shows that every square on this gourd leaf has become larger, indicating that the entire leaf is growing.

A stem grows solely from its tip. As the cells mature, some cells will harden, providing protection. Middle cells will become part of the xylem and phloem.

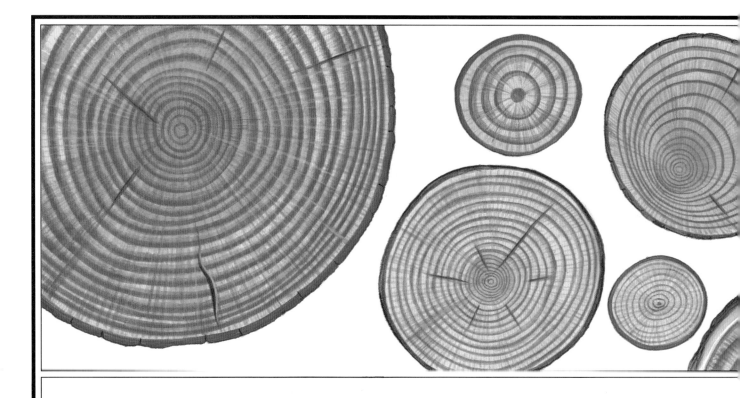

2
Roots and Stems

A plant is about 90 percent water, but it loses large amounts of water through evaporation from its leaves. One corn plant, for example, can lose 50 gallons of water over its four-month life. As a result, plants require a steady supply of water to grow. To get water, a plant develops an underground network of roots that allows it to tap into the soil for its water needs. As a plant grows so does its need for water, and its network of lateral roots will spread farther from the stem. Many plants have a main root, called a taproot, a large single root that grows nearly straight down.

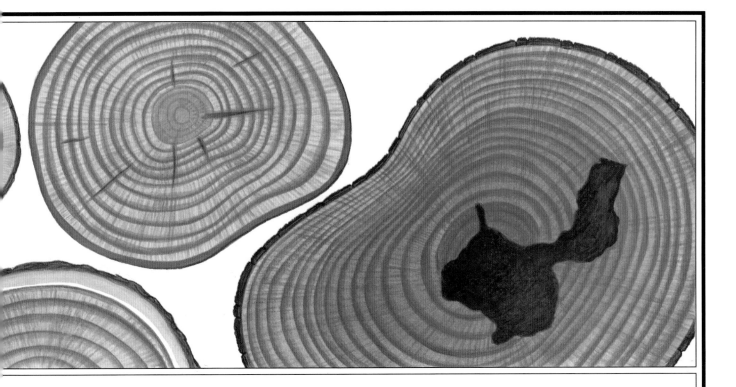

Once a plant's roots absorb water from the soil, its stem must carry the water to the branches and leaves. This task falls to the xylem, a ring of hollow tubes that extends from the roots, through the stem, and out to every branch and leaf. The xylem lies near the surface of the stem. In a tree, for example, the xylem forms a band just below the bark. The xylem is made of dead cells linked end to end like a giant straw. A force known as the water potential draws water up through the xylem from wet roots to dry leaves.

Roots and stems have a second important role: They support the plant as it grows. The network of roots anchors the plant in the soil, while the stem provides the strength to keep the branches and leaves from collapsing.

As a tree grows, its roots spread farther from the trunk to reach more water *(below)*. A tree's trunk grows larger, too, providing more support and water-carrying capacity. This growth produces the rings in a tree trunk *(above)*. Each ring represents one year of growth.

How Does Water Get to the Treetop?

In an act that seems to defy gravity, water rises from the roots buried underground to the leaves, which may be as much as 300 feet above ground. There is no pump, like an animal's heart, to push water through a plant. Instead, several physical forces work together to carry water upward for great distances without forcing the plant to use even the slightest bit of its own energy.

The key force driving the water is known as the water potential. When a wet and a dry place are joined by a tube of water, the water flows toward the dry area. In plants, roots are surrounded by moisture. A leaf, however, loses water continually through pores in its surface. This is called transpiration. As a result of transpiration, leaves are always drier than roots, and water always moves on its own from roots to leaves.

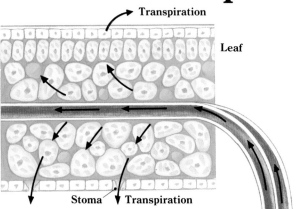

Leaf structure and water flow

The epidermis, a layer of tightly packed cells, covers the leaf and reduces evaporation. Most of the water lost from a leaf evaporates through the stomas, small pores that also admit carbon dioxide.

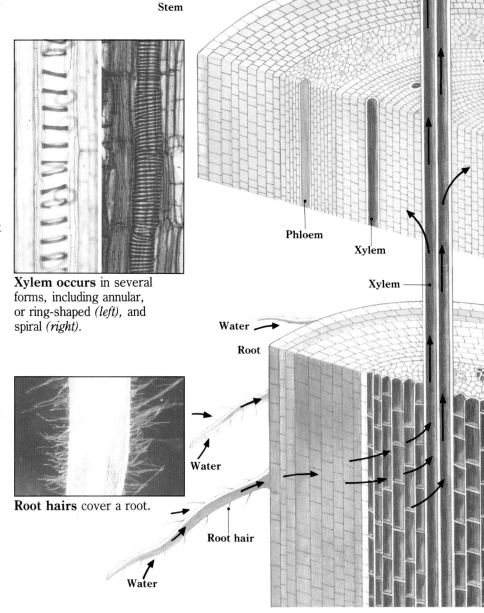

The stem

A plant stem is made of several layers *(far right),* each with a specific function. The outer two layers *(white and yellow)* protect the stem from injury and reduce water loss. The next layer *(blue)* contains the phloem, live cells connected end to end in long tubes. The phloem transports proteins and sugars made in the leaves to the stem and roots. The xylem *(red tubes),* in the next layer of cells, carries water in the opposite direction. Cells in the center of the stem, called the pith, store food.

Xylem occurs in several forms, including annular, or ring-shaped *(left),* and spiral *(right).*

Root hairs

A magnified section of a root *(right)* shows the two components most involved in absorbing and transporting water. The fuzzy strands are the root hairs. Each hair is one long, thin cell that absorbs water. Once water enters a root hair, it passes through the outer layers of cells to the vascular bundle, the band in the center of the root. The vascular bundle contains both xylem and phloem. Water passes into the xylem and begins its journey upward.

Root hairs cover a root.

Moving water in a plant

Transpiration

Transpiration

Water always travels from wet to dry regions. Since air is drier than a leaf, water evaporates from the leaf through its stomas into the air. Transpiration also creates a water potential between the leaves and the roots that draws water up through the xylem.

Stomas

Droplets from root pressure

Cohesion

Water is able to climb hundreds of feet in a tree because water molecules stick to each other and to the walls of the xylem tubes. This phenomenon is called cohesion. In the illustration at right, water evaporating from the top of a tube creates a water potential that pulls water from the beaker. Without cohesion, the water would barely rise. Cohesion increases as the diameter of the tube decreases.

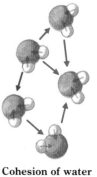

Cohesion of water

Root pressure

Root tissue absorbs more and more water and minerals as it grows. As water in the roots increases, pressure builds up, forcing water into the xylem and up into the stem. Root pressure is highest at night, and it can cause water droplets to seep from plant leaves *(top, far right)*.

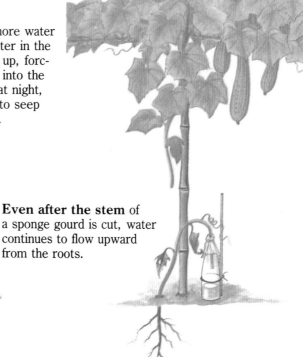

Even after the stem of a sponge gourd is cut, water continues to flow upward from the roots.

Why Do Some Roots Grow on Top?

Most plants send their roots into the soil, both to anchor themselves and to gather moisture. Not all plants grow in the ground, however, and such plants have roots adapted to their unusual environments. Air plants, or epiphytes, use their roots to cling to tree trunks and to absorb moisture directly from the air. Mistletoe and other parasitic plants dig their roots into some plants to obtain water and nutrients.

Certain plants with roots beneath the ground produce aboveground roots, too. Vines such as ivy use aerial roots to support themselves as they climb. Mangrove trees live in swamps, where the ground is covered with water. To get oxygen for their submerged roots, they grow additional roots that rise above the water.

Root systems

Aerial roots. Many small plants growing in dense tropical forests are epiphytes, plants that grow on tree trunks without harming them. Wind and birds deposit epiphyte seeds onto a tree trunk. There the seed sprouts thick roots that anchor the plant to the tree. The small hitchhiker is then closer to sunlight without needing a long stem. A layer of dead cells on the roots absorbs water from the tropical air.

Several members of the orchid family, including the *Neofinetia falcata* shown at right, are epiphytes.

The bald cypress, a native of North American swamps, sends brown knobby knee roots above ground to get oxygen for its waterlogged roots.

Respiratory roots. Roots need oxygen to survive, which creates a problem for trees that live in swamps and along tropical coasts, where the soil is wet and contains little oxygen. To get the oxygen they need, trees such as the cypress send root projections above ground. These respiratory roots have soft, spongy tissues, through which air travels easily to the roots below ground.

Mistletoe sends its roots into a tree to obtain water and minerals.

Parasitic roots. Some plants are parasites. They cannot make their own food or get their own water. Instead, they send their roots, called haustoria, into the stem and roots of another plant and draw out the food and water they need.

Aquatic roots. Plants that float on water have long, thin roots that hang in the water. The space between roots cells is large, making it easier for these cells to absorb oxygen directly from the water.

Duckweed is a small floating plant with roots that hang in the water.

Ficus tree

Buttress root

Support root

The climbing roots of ivy, a vine, attach the plant to its support.

Support and buttress roots. Plants that grow in soft or wet soils, such as ficus trees *(above),* use buttress roots to help keep themselves erect. The roots grow from nodes on the tree trunk. Corn plants use support roots *(left).*

Climbing root. Some plants have weak stems, so they use sticky roots to climb above the ground. These roots avoid the sun by growing into cracks on bark and in buildings.

Corn plant

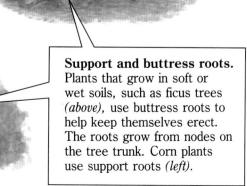

23

What Causes Growth Rings in Trees?

In the temperate regions of the world such as North America and Europe, trees grow in spurts—fast in the spring, slower in summer and autumn. In winter, they do not grow at all. This seasonal pattern repeats itself every year and produces growth rings. Such rings are easily seen on any tree stump *(right)*. Each ring represents one year's production of new xylem. The lighter bands represent the growth spurt of spring, while the darker bands mark the slower growth of summer and autumn. As a tree ages, the cells in the older rings become inactive, then fill up with resins, gums, and oils, and harden, forming what is known as the heartwood. This provides most of a tree's strength and is the part used to make lumber.

The growth rings of the tree at left show it to be about 60 years old.

Xylem and wood

4th year

3d year

2d year

1st year

Pith

A living climate record

Growth rings not only reveal a tree's age but also record what the weather was like in each year of its life. A wide growth ring indicates that rainfall was plentiful, allowing the tree to grow rapidly. A thin ring indicates drought, when there was little water to spur growth. Sometimes growth rings are lopsided, growing faster and wider on the south side, where there is plenty of sunlight *(right)*. Fossil tree stumps give evidence that the Earth's climate has changed many times over the last several hundred million years.

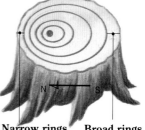

Narrow rings   Broad rings

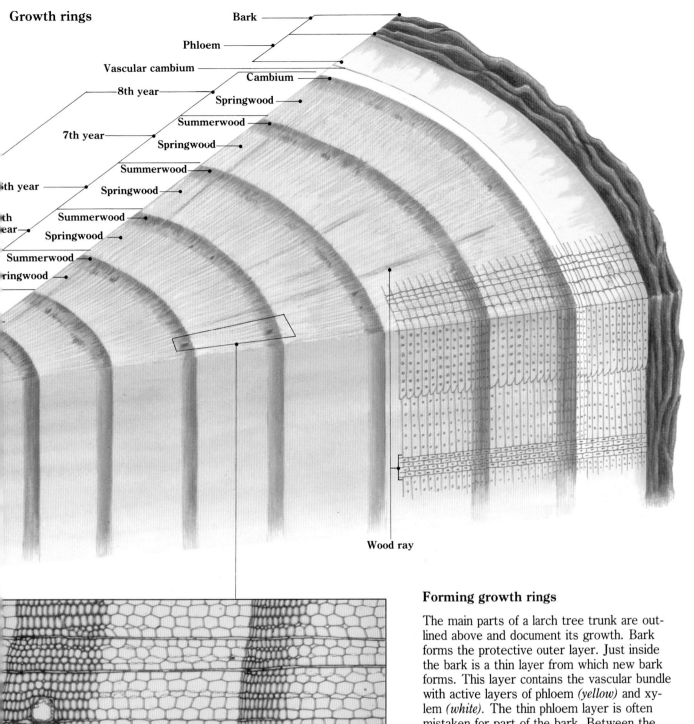

Growth rings

Bark

Phloem

Vascular cambium

Cambium

8th year

Springwood

Summerwood

7th year

Springwood

Summerwood

Springwood

6th year

Summerwood

5th year

Springwood

Summerwood

Springwood

Wood ray

A cross section shows summer and spring growth.

Missing growth rings

Trees growing in the world's tropical regions, such as the Philippine mahogany, often lack growth rings. A mystery? No. There are no distinct seasons in equatorial climates, so trees grow at about the same rate all year. Some tropical areas have wet and dry seasons, and the trees growing there may form rings. However, these rings are not reliable indicators of a tree's age because they may not form each year.

Forming growth rings

The main parts of a larch tree trunk are outlined above and document its growth. Bark forms the protective outer layer. Just inside the bark is a thin layer from which new bark forms. This layer contains the vascular bundle with active layers of phloem *(yellow)* and xylem *(white)*. The thin phloem layer is often mistaken for part of the bark. Between the phloem and the xylem lies the cork cambium *(green)*. Another cambium layer, one cell thick *(thin brown line)*, is virtually invisible, yet this is where the tree trunk is growing. Cambium cells divide constantly during the growth season. Some move toward the outside of the tree and become phloem. Others split off toward the tree's center and become xylem.

In spring, the cambium grows rapidly to meet the heavy demands for transporting water and stored food through the tree as it produces leaves. The new cells the tree produces are large, interspersed with even larger vessels that transport water *(left)*. In summer and autumn, growth slows, and the cells become smaller. One band each of large and small cells produces one growth ring.

Why Do Sycamores Have Spotted Bark?

Sycamore trees are known for their spotted, multicolored trunks *(right)*. This pattern occurs because sycamores, like all other trees, shed their bark as they grow larger. What makes sycamores different is that their bark peels off in patches. Bark is the dead outer layer of cork, a band of waterproof, airtight cells that protects the tree from insects, disease, water loss, and sudden temperature change. As a tree trunk grows in diameter, the cork-and-bark layer must also expand to keep its protective seal intact. Since the bark itself is dead, it cannot grow. Instead, it peels or cracks. This gives bark its textured appearance. Cells in the cork cambium do grow, however, and so the cork can expand to accommodate the tree's larger girth.

Bark structure

Bark is made of dead cork cells formed from the dividing cells in the cork cambium, as shown below.

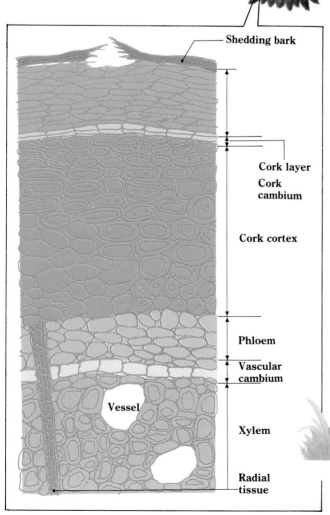

Shedding bark

Cork layer

Cork cambium

Cork cortex

Phloem

Vascular cambium

Vessel

Xylem

Radial tissue

Sycamore. As a sycamore grows, the bark flakes away in patches. This reveals younger, lighter-colored bark.

Cork cambium

Tree trunks grow larger because cambium cells grow and divide throughout a tree's life. As the cells inside the trunk increase in number, pressure on the outside layers increases too, causing the layers to expand and crack. When this happens, cells in the cork cambium layer respond by growing and dividing to fill gaps in the cracked outer layer. And the protective layer of bark expands as the tree trunk grows *(below)*.

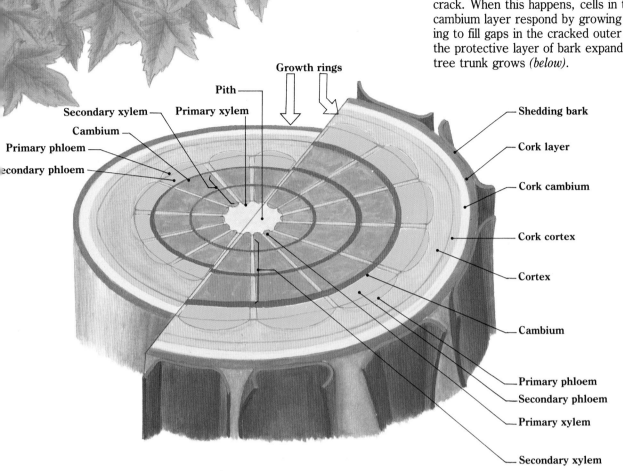

Growth rings

Pith

Secondary xylem

Cambium

Primary xylem

Primary phloem

Secondary phloem

Shedding bark

Cork layer

Cork cambium

Cork cortex

Cortex

Cambium

Primary phloem

Secondary phloem

Primary xylem

Secondary xylem

Lenticels

Some tree trunks are covered with small raised bumps *(right)*. These are lenticels, pores that allow the tree trunk's tissue to breathe. The cells in a lenticel are loosely packed *(far right)* and allow oxygen and carbon dioxide to pass through the bark layer easily.

Cherry tree lenticels   **Red-berry** elder bark and cross section of a lenticel

Different types of bark

One way to identify a tree is to examine the patterns in its bark. These patterns depend on the way a particular species of tree expands as it grows. Some species, for example, shed their bark in strips, others in patches. The cracks can be deep or shallow, regular or irregular, with a network of fissures and ribs.

Scaled. Red pine   **Fibrous.** Cedar   **Barred.** Japanese oak   **Granular.** Zelkova   **Ringed.** White birch

What Are Thorns, Prickles, and Spines?

Plants such as roses and cacti protect themselves from hungry beasts with sharp, woody growths. On a rose, these growths are commonly called thorns, but they are really prickles that arise from the outer layer of the stem. On a cactus, the growths are called spines, and they are a form of leaf. Other plants with spines include holly, where the spines grow from the tips of the leaves, and stinging nettles, whose spines break and release a poison when touched. True thorns are modified stems, as in the honey locust and hawthorn. In some cases thorns sprout leaves.

Roses. Few plants are as prized as the rose, the "queen of flowers." The Chinese first cultivated roses because of their beauty some 5,000 years ago. During the Middle Ages, roses were grown for medicinal purposes.

Rose defense

A rose prickle is part of the plant's outer layer, or epidermis, as shown at right. Unconnected to the inner parts of the stem, it peels away easily with the epidermis *(below)*.

Rose prickle

A rose prickle is a woody outgrowth of the epidermis.

Prickles and spines

The sharp growths on a rose bush *(above, right)* and on a false acacia tree *(right)* may look like thorns, but they are not. Rose thorns are actually prickles, a woody outgrowth from the plant's epidermis. Those on a false acacia are called spines, which are modified leaves.

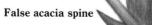

False acacia spine

False acacia. This flowering tree *(above)* has two sharp spines below every bud *(left)*.

28

Plant modification

Root, stem, and leaf are the three basic parts of every plant, but in many cases these parts grow into structures that bear little resemblance to the original organ. This adaptation turns leaves into spines or tendrils. Different parts of a plant that arise from the same organ are called homologous features. The spines of a false acacia, the tendrils of a pea plant, and the edible part of an onion are all homologous, since each is a modified leaf. In some cases, two plants may have features that look the same or have the same function, but that nevertheless developed from different organs. These are called analogous parts. An onion, potato, and sweet potato seem similar, but an onion is a modified leaf, a potato is a modified stem, and a sweet potato is a swollen root. In the same way, the tendrils of a pea and ivy are analogous, since the pea tendril is actually a leaf, and the ivy tendril is part of the stem.

Homology and analogy in nature

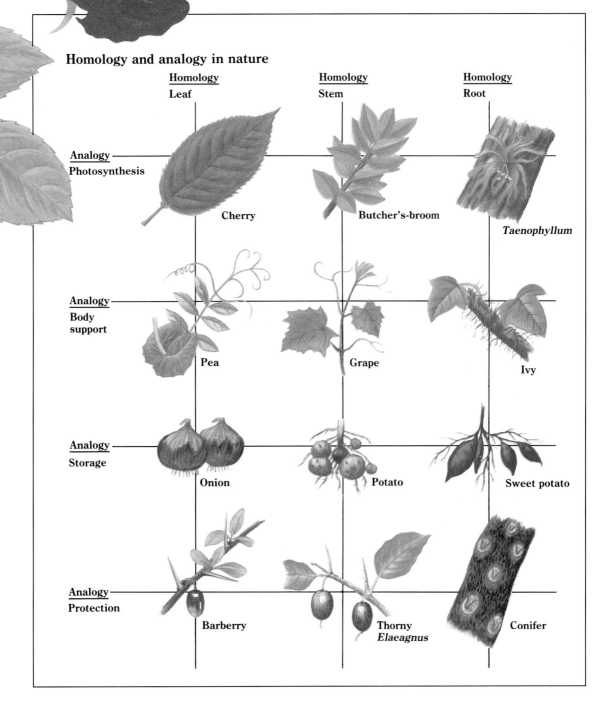

	Homology Leaf	Homology Stem	Homology Root
Analogy Photosynthesis	Cherry	Butcher's-broom	*Taenophyllum*
Analogy Body support	Pea	Grape	Ivy
Analogy Storage	Onion	Potato	Sweet potato
Analogy Protection	Barberry	Thorny *Elaeagnus*	Conifer

How Do Cucumber Tendrils Coil?

Cucumbers and other vine plants grow by climbing a pole or another plant, and they use tendrils to cling to their support. The tendrils of a cucumber are modified stems, and their tips are sensitive to contact. The illustration on the far right shows how the tendrils reach out. When a tendril touches a pole, for example, it begins to curl around it. Within 14 hours the tendril is firmly attached to the support. About a day after first making contact, the tendril begins coiling, or twining, from both ends at the same time. The coils form around a spot in the middle of the tendril called the reverse twining point. Twenty-four hours later, the tendril is tightly coiled.

Some vines, such as the grape, have sucker-like pads at the tips of their tendrils. These stick to their support, rather than wrapping around it. But after making contact, these tendrils coil as well. Other climbing plants, including ivy, use modified roots to support themselves. Unlike tendrils, these do not form coils.

Pea tendril. Like cucumbers, peas, of the legume family *(right)*, use tendrils to support themselves as they climb. But a cucumber's tendrils are modified stems, while the pea's tendrils are related to leaves.

Cucumbers are members of the gourd family. They are natives of India, where they have been grown for 3,000 years. Over the years cucumber varieties have spread to nearly every country of the world. All cucumbers are vines that use tendrils for support. The edible part, or fruit, of the serpent cucumber grows up to 3 feet long, while the Sikkim cucumber, from the Himalayas, can have a diameter of 6 inches.

Nature's springs

Straight tendrils might be able to support a plant as well as coiled ones, but coils do have their advantages. Coils *(far right)* draw the plant closer to its support, so it can bear more of the plant's weight. Coiled tendrils can also stretch, enabling them to withstand a strong wind that would snap a straight tendril.

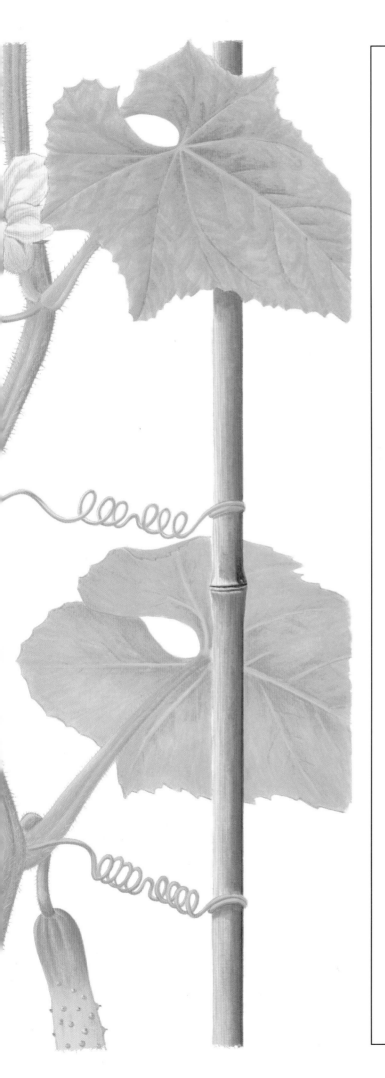

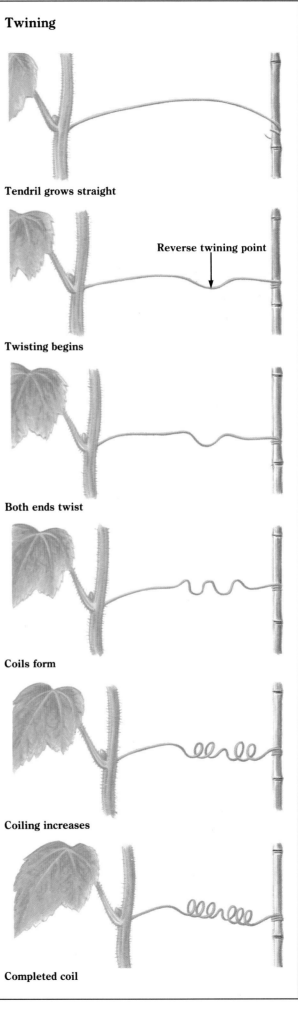

Twining

Tendril grows straight

Twisting begins

Reverse twining point

Both ends twist

Coils form

Coiling increases

Completed coil

How Can Bamboo Grow So Fast?

The fastest-growing plants in the world may be the more than 500 species of bamboo. Some bamboos produce culms, or stalks, that grow 16 inches a day and may reach 120 feet in height when fully grown. Bamboo grows rapidly because it grows in several places at the same time.

All plants grow when cells in a tissue called meristem divide and become larger. But in plants other than bamboo, meristem exists only at the tips of stems. In a bamboo culm, however, each node contains meristem, and since there may be 60 nodes on one bamboo shoot, it can grow 60 times faster than other plants. As the meristem at each node produces new cells, the distance between neighboring nodes increases. A sheath covers each node, protecting it from damage and from exposure to sunlight—factors that stop bamboo meristem from growing. As the bamboo grows, the sheath may fall off or be eaten by browsing animals. Growth then stops at that particular node. The nodes near the tip of the bamboo shoot produce branches that also sprout leaves. After decades of growth, the plant suddenly blooms and dies.

Internodal growth

The illustration below shows the structure of a bamboo stem near its tip. New cells grow at each node. The space between each pair of nodes, called the internode, increases as the plant grows (right). This manner of growth produces the bamboo's hollow, jointed stem with a solid disk at each node.

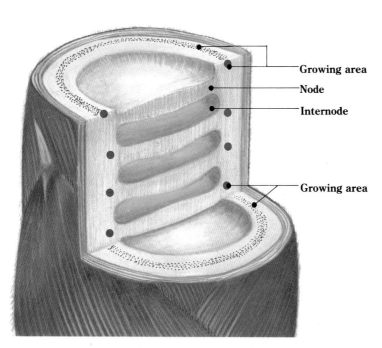

Growing area
Node
Internode

Growing area

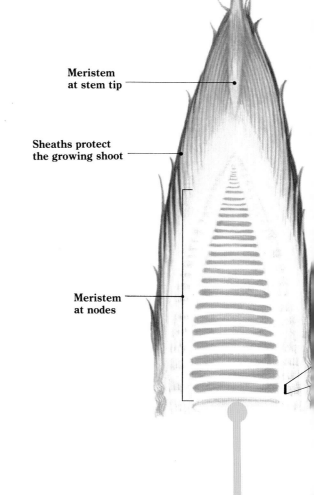

Meristem at stem tip

Sheaths protect the growing shoot

Meristem at nodes

Grass or tree?

Bamboo is hard like wood, and it continues growing to great heights over the course of many years. In that respect it may seem to be a tree. But actually, bamboo is a member of the grass family, and like other grasses, bamboo dies when it blooms, although flowering may occur only every 10 to 120 years.

Bamboo stays slim

Bamboo, like all grasses, is a monocotyledon, meaning that its seeds contain one seed leaf. Unlike tree trunks, stems of monocotyledons do not have a cambium layer and do not produce new xylem and phloem layers each year. As a result, bamboo does not get much thicker as it ages but mostly grows taller.

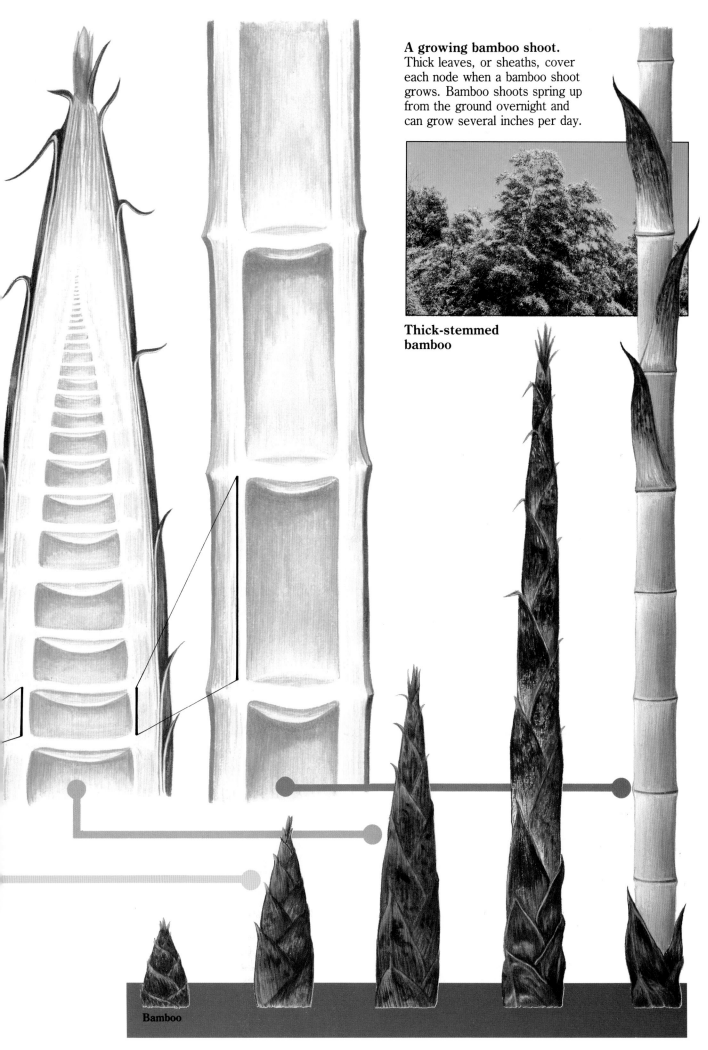

A growing bamboo shoot.
Thick leaves, or sheaths, cover each node when a bamboo shoot grows. Bamboo shoots spring up from the ground overnight and can grow several inches per day.

Thick-stemmed bamboo

Bamboo

3
Structure and Function of Leaves

Every tree on the planet owes its continued existence to its leaves. Although widely varied in shape and size, all leaves are similar in function. Their common goal is to produce food through photosynthesis, a process that converts water and carbon dioxide into sugars that sustain the plant's life. Leaves also share a similar internal structure, with great numbers of chloroplasts *(pages 6-7)* lined up to absorb the proper amount of sunlight for their own level of photosynthesis. Leaves also have stomas, or pores, which serve as vents to the outside atmosphere and aid in

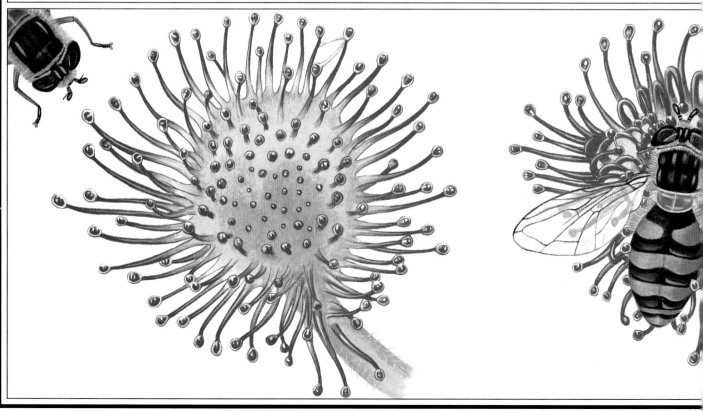

regulating the amount of water coursing through the plant. Leaves control not only the amount of water in plants but also the power with which the roots absorb moisture. The leaves, whose life span may be as short as six months or as long as several years, even serve a purpose after they have died. When the leaves of a deciduous tree or an evergreen fall to the ground, they take with them some of the waste products the tree has produced during the leaves' lifetime. The fallen leaves then decay and add essential humus to the soil. But it is not only the tree that owes its ex-

istence to these miniature food factories. Everyone has a stake in the future of leaves. That is because one of the by-products of the process of photosynthesis is oxygen, without which no animal—including humans—could survive.

In many regions, the leaves of deciduous trees *(above)* are beautiful harbingers of seasonal changes. On other plants, such as the insect-eating sundew *(below)*, leaves play a more aggressive role.

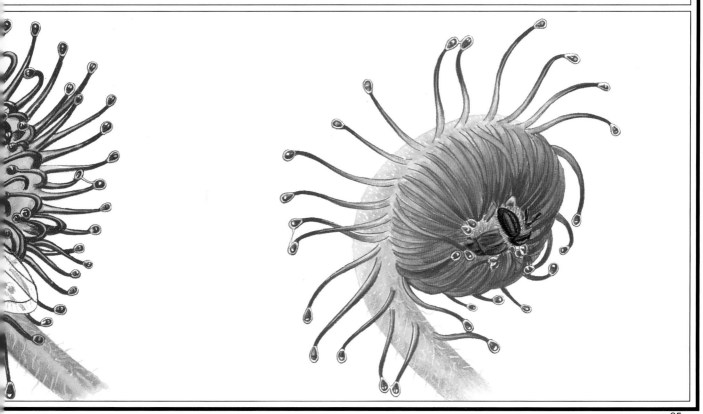

Why Do Leaves Differ in Each Plant?

Plants grow and maintain themselves through photosynthesis, a process in which their leaves collect sunlight to convert water and carbon dioxide into sugars. Since not all plants are exposed to sunlight in the same way, leaves have different shapes to accommodate each plant's individual needs. Some plants, for example, push their stems upward to rise above other plants and compete for sunlight. Others, such as ferns, which grow close to the forest floor, spread their branches wide to get the right amount of light.

Even leaves that seem to be haphazardly arranged have a specific design for receiving precious light. Each one is attached to the stem at an angle and location that allows it to receive the light it needs and to avoid as much as possible any overlapping with other leaves. This special way in which leaves attach to plant stems is called phyllotaxy, or leaf arrangement. Different groupings—most commonly alternate, opposite, and whorled leaf arrangements—are found throughout the plant world.

Sunflower leaf arrangement

The phyllotaxy, or arrangement of leaves on a plant stem, is expressed as a fraction. The sunflower below and at right, an example of a leaf arrangement called alternate phyllotaxy, has a phyllotaxy of ⅜. This means that eight leaves make three spiral circuits around the stem, counted from the bottom leaf and beginning anew with the ninth leaf directly above the first one.

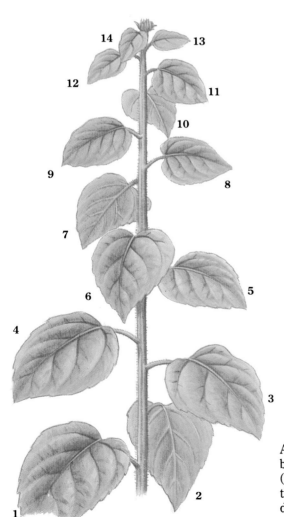

A leaf's degree of divergence is calculated by multiplying its leaf arrangement by 360° (representing one turn around the stem). Thus the sunflower, with its phyllotaxy of ⅜, has a degree of divergence from leaf to leaf of 135°.

How leaves are arranged

The points at which leaves are attached to the stem of a plant are called nodes. If there is just one leaf at each node, the arrangement is called alternate phyllotaxy *(below, left)*. If there is a pair of leaves at each node, the arrangement is referred to as opposite phyllotaxy *(below, center)*. If more than two leaves are attached to a single node, the arrangement is called whorled phyllotaxy *(below, right)*.

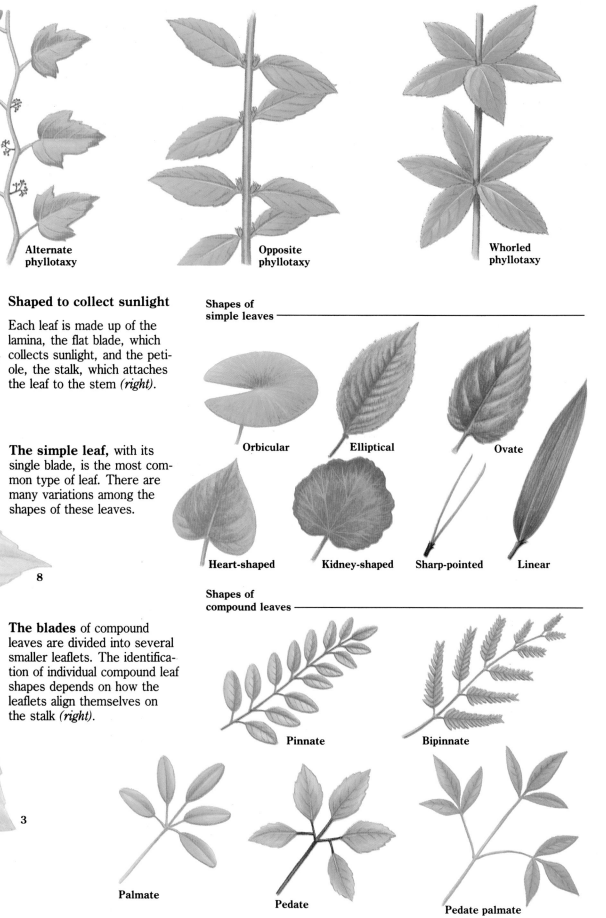

Alternate phyllotaxy

Opposite phyllotaxy

Whorled phyllotaxy

Shaped to collect sunlight

Each leaf is made up of the lamina, the flat blade, which collects sunlight, and the petiole, the stalk, which attaches the leaf to the stem *(right)*.

The simple leaf, with its single blade, is the most common type of leaf. There are many variations among the shapes of these leaves.

Shapes of simple leaves

Orbicular

Elliptical

Ovate

Heart-shaped

Kidney-shaped

Sharp-pointed

Linear

Shapes of compound leaves

The blades of compound leaves are divided into several smaller leaflets. The identification of individual compound leaf shapes depends on how the leaflets align themselves on the stalk *(right)*.

Pinnate

Bipinnate

Palmate

Pedate

Pedate palmate

5

8

11

3

Can Plants Breathe?

Plants do breathe, but they do it in their own special way. Unlike animals, which take in oxygen and expel carbon dioxide, plants handle their gas exchange in two different steps, called respiration and photosynthesis. In respiration, plants take in oxygen and expel carbon dioxide, oxidizing nutrients along the way. In photosynthesis, the process by which plants manufacture their own food, plants require sunlight and certain other raw materials. One of the most important of these ingredients is carbon dioxide, which the plant takes from the air through its leaves. Using sunshine as its energy source, photosynthesis combines the carbon dioxide with water, usually taken in through the roots, to produce simple sugars and oxygen. The process produces more oxygen than the plant can use. At night, when the absence of sunlight halts photosynthesis, the plant discharges this excess oxygen from the stomas, or leaf pores. In this fashion, oxygen from plants sustains humankind and all other life on earth.

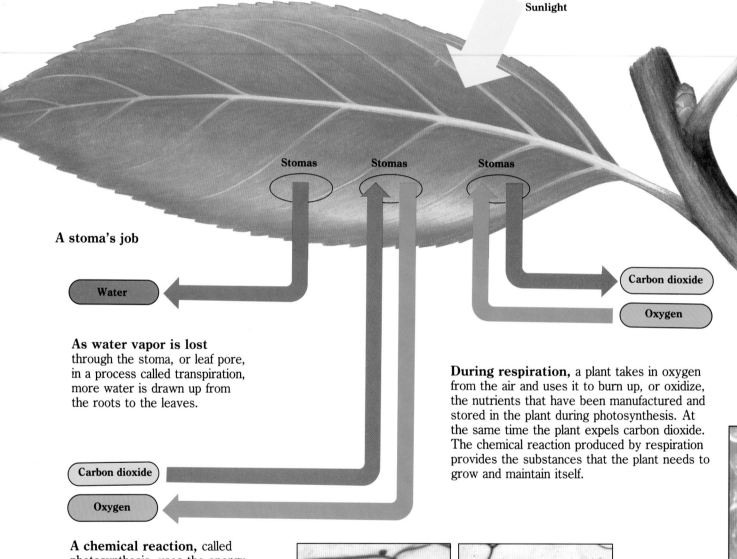

Sunlight

Stomas   Stomas   Stomas

A stoma's job

Water

Carbon dioxide

Oxygen

As water vapor is lost through the stoma, or leaf pore, in a process called transpiration, more water is drawn up from the roots to the leaves.

Carbon dioxide

Oxygen

During respiration, a plant takes in oxygen from the air and uses it to burn up, or oxidize, the nutrients that have been manufactured and stored in the plant during photosynthesis. At the same time the plant expels carbon dioxide. The chemical reaction produced by respiration provides the substances that the plant needs to grow and maintain itself.

A chemical reaction, called photosynthesis, uses the energy of sunlight to produce oxygen and to synthesize a simple sugar called d-glucose from the carbon dioxide in the air. Since the process requires sunlight, photosynthesis cannot occur at night. When photosynthesis ends for the day, the plant releases its excess oxygen.

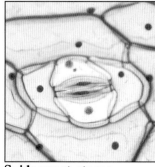

Spiderwort stoma   **Sedum stomas**

Cross section of a leaf

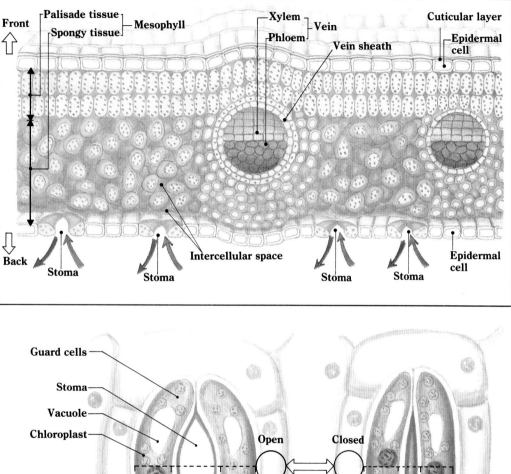

Stomas, the openings on the front and back of each leaf, assist the gas exchange in respiration and photosynthesis, and also in transpiration. The gases are spread throughout the internal organs of the leaf through intercellular spaces such as the mesophyll, consisting of the palisade and spongy tissues.

The stoma, located in the plant's epidermis, is a small hole surrounded by two kidney-shaped guard cells. There can be as many as 200 stomas, or more, in an area no larger than the head of a pin.

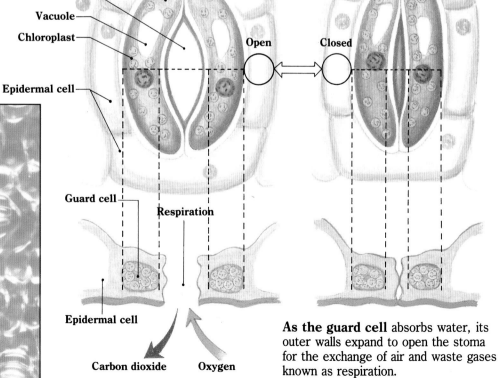

As the guard cell absorbs water, its outer walls expand to open the stoma for the exchange of air and waste gases known as respiration.

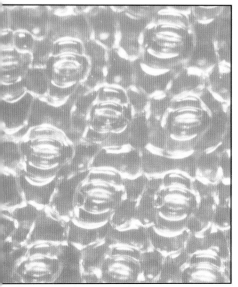

Dense areas reveal the stomas.

What Causes Leaves to Change Color?

In the autumn, a leaf goes through many changes that alter its color. First, as the days grow shorter and the temperature drops, an abscission, or separation, layer forms at the base of the leaf stalk. This interrupts the flow of sugar made in photosynthesis. As a result, sugar is trapped in the leaf. In maple and sumac leaves, the sugar produces a bright red pigment called anthocyanin—the name for any of the class of pigments that give flowers colors in the blue to red range. At the same time, decomposing chlorophyll causes the leaf's green color to fade, so the red becomes visible. Yellow autumn leaves get their color from a yellow pigment called carotene.

The structure of a leaf

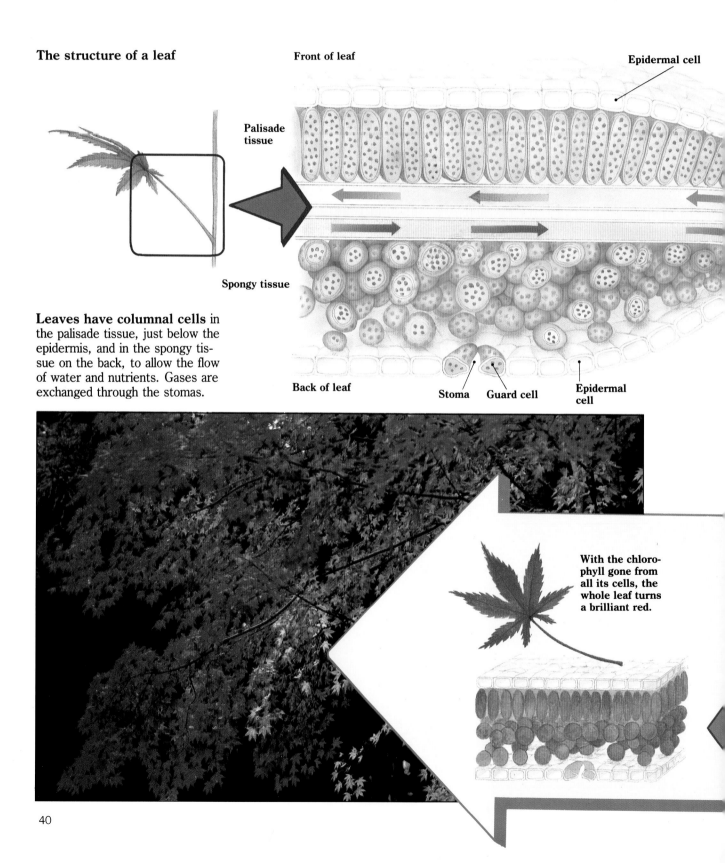

Front of leaf

Epidermal cell

Palisade tissue

Spongy tissue

Back of leaf

Stoma   Guard cell   Epidermal cell

Leaves have columnal cells in the palisade tissue, just below the epidermis, and in the spongy tissue on the back, to allow the flow of water and nutrients. Gases are exchanged through the stomas.

With the chlorophyll gone from all its cells, the whole leaf turns a brilliant red.

Preparing for separation

As autumn temperatures get lower and the days become shorter, tree roots send less water and fewer nutrients to the leaves. As a result, leaf activity slows down, and the soft cells form a small colony called the abscission, or separation, layer across the stalk *(far right)*. When this layer grows, it forms an enzyme that decomposes the stalk's cell walls, weakens the leaf's attachment to the tree, and eventually causes the leaf to fall.

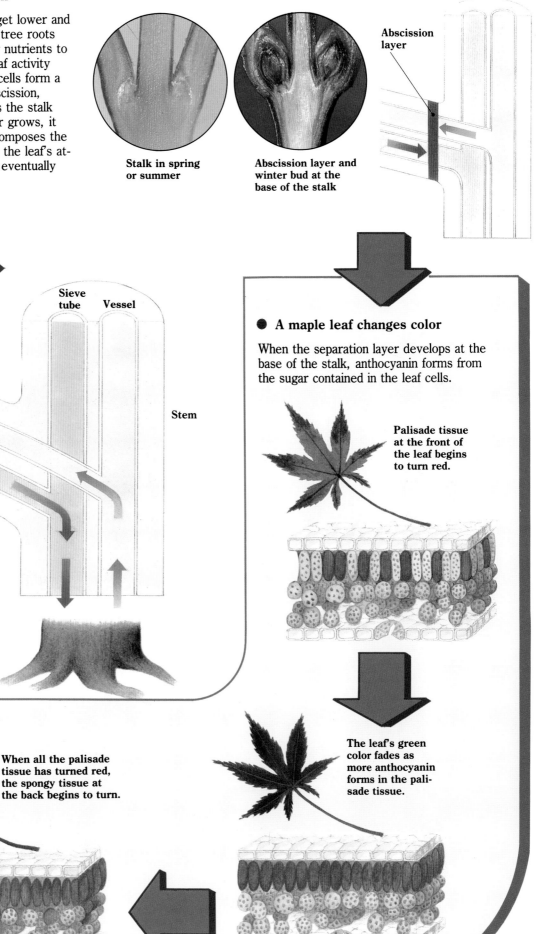

Stalk in spring or summer

Abscission layer and winter bud at the base of the stalk

Abscission layer

Stalk

Sieve tube   Vessel

Stem

The water absorbed by the roots flows through the vessels to saturate the whole tree. When the water reaches the leaves, it transpires out of the plant through stomas on the back of the leaves.

● **A maple leaf changes color**

When the separation layer develops at the base of the stalk, anthocyanin forms from the sugar contained in the leaf cells.

Palisade tissue at the front of the leaf begins to turn red.

The leaf's green color fades as more anthocyanin forms in the palisade tissue.

When all the palisade tissue has turned red, the spongy tissue at the back begins to turn.

41

Why Do Leaves Fall in the Autumn?

Shedding leaves is one way for trees to conserve their water supply during the harsh winter months. These leaf-losing, or deciduous, trees have leaves that are thin *(below)* compared with the leaves of evergreens *(box, opposite)*. The thinner leaves lose a great deal more water through transpiration than do the thick evergreen leaves. So, in the winter when root activity and water absorption decrease, the deciduous trees drop their leaves to keep water loss at a minimum. Discarding their leaves also helps them dispose of toxic or waste products, such as calcium and silicon, which have accumulated during the summer.

The leaves of the poplar tree *(left)* have flattened stalks, which cause the leaves to flutter easily. This aids greatly in transpiration and allows the poplar to grow in wet ground. The name "poplar" comes from the Greek word *papaillo,* which means "to shake."

The mechanics of defoliation

The cooler, shorter days of autumn restrict the flow of water and nutrients, causing a decrease in leaf activity. Soon colonies of soft cells form around the base of the stalk. This zone, called the abscission, or separation, layer, produces an enzyme called pectin, which dissolves the stalk's cell walls and causes the leaf to detach. When the leaf falls, a cork layer quickly forms over the point of detachment to protect the severed stem.

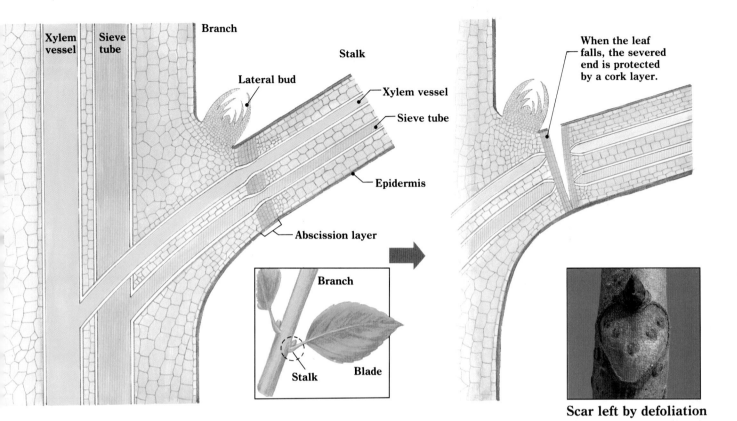

Scar left by defoliation

Not all trees defoliate

Some deciduous trees do not shed their leaves in winter. The dead leaves of several oaks *(below)*, for example, remain on their branches throughout winter. In the spring, replacement buds push the old oak leaves off the tree. Other deciduous trees, such as the chestnut, also hang onto their leaves in winter. Some beech trees, the ones that originated in southern climates, never developed the ability to produce abscission layers and therefore cannot shed their leaves effectively.

Quercus borealis   *Quercus variabilis*

How an evergreen defoliates

Trees that retain green leaves all year round are called evergreens. This does not mean, however, that they keep the same leaves year after year. Unlike a deciduous tree, which loses its leaves all at once, the evergreen sheds and replaces leaves continuously. On the average, an evergreen leaf lives for three to four years, although the life span varies greatly from one plant family to another. Trees of the pine family *(below, left)*, for example, may keep leaves for up to nine years. The life span of a rhododendron leaf, on the other hand, may be as short as six months.

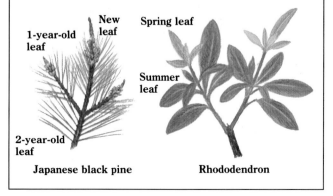

Japanese black pine   Rhododendron

What Makes Mimosa Leaves Curl?

When disturbed, the leaves of the mimosa curl up and the stalk bends downward. This response to outside stimuli is called nastic movement and is caused by a sudden change in water balance. The mimosa, native to the grasslands of South America, exhibits two kinds of nastic movement. One type, called haptonasty, is a reaction to touch. The other type, called photonasty, is a reaction to light. Both reactions occur at a swelling, called a leaf cushion, at the base of the stalk and at the point of attachment of the leaflets. Upon the slightest touch, the swelling drains its stored water and causes the leaves or stalks to droop.

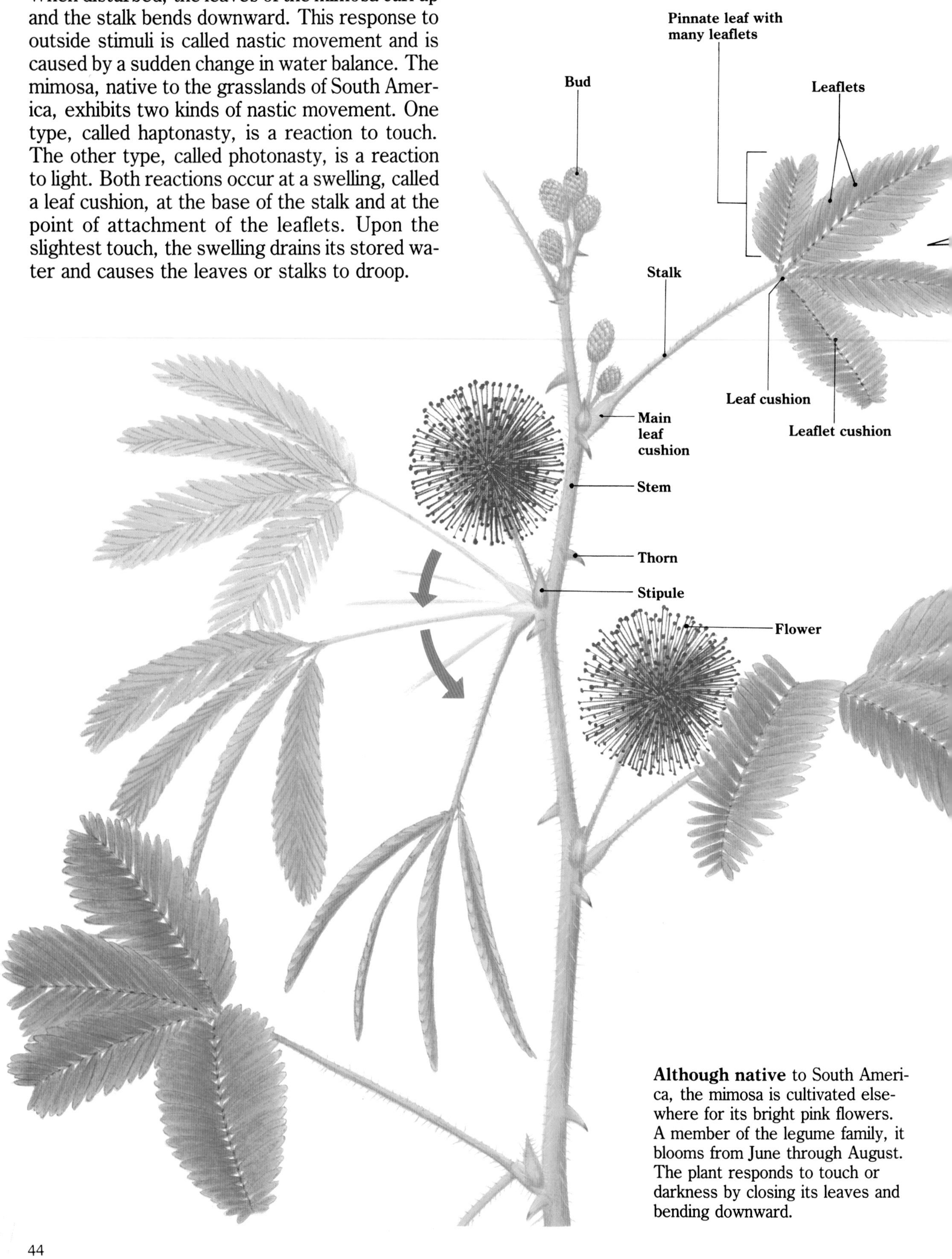

Pinnate leaf with many leaflets

Bud

Leaflets

Stalk

Leaf cushion

Leaflet cushion

Main leaf cushion

Stem

Thorn

Stipule

Flower

Although native to South America, the mimosa is cultivated elsewhere for its bright pink flowers. A member of the legume family, it blooms from June through August. The plant responds to touch or darkness by closing its leaves and bending downward.

Reacting to touch

When the mimosa is disturbed, the liquid-filled motor cells in its leaf cushion leak water into the space between the cells. This loss of water pressure causes the leaflets to fold and the leaves to droop and wilt, all of which occurs in a matter of seconds. But it takes up to several hours for the mimosa to recover. The plants are so exquisitely sensitive that they were once believed to have an animal-like nervous system.

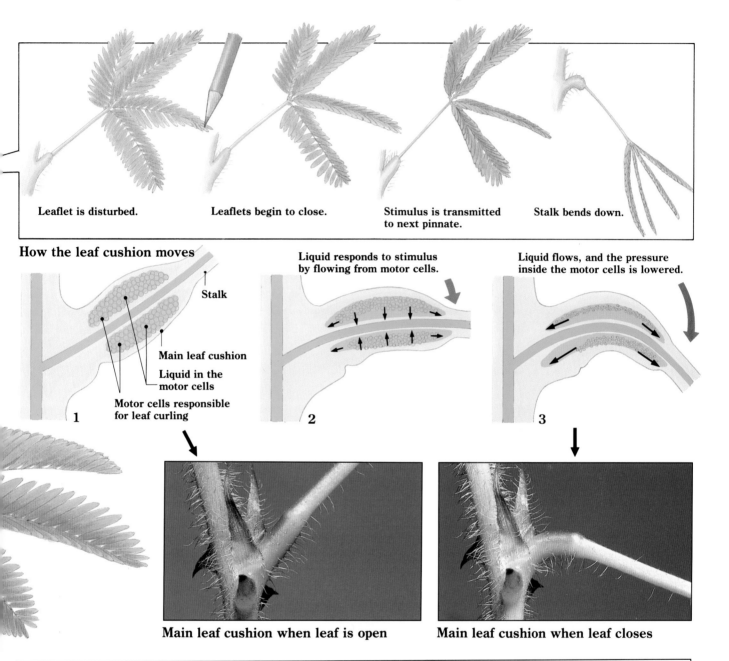

Leaflet is disturbed.

Leaflets begin to close.

Stimulus is transmitted to next pinnate.

Stalk bends down.

How the leaf cushion moves

Stalk

Main leaf cushion

Liquid in the motor cells

Motor cells responsible for leaf curling

1

Liquid responds to stimulus by flowing from motor cells.

2

Liquid flows, and the pressure inside the motor cells is lowered.

3

Main leaf cushion when leaf is open

Main leaf cushion when leaf closes

The mimosa's sleeping posture

In addition to its closing and drooping response to physical touch, the mimosa is extremely sensitive to light. This is true of some grasses and herbs as well, such as the wood sorrel, shown at far right. The leaves of the plant close up shortly after dark and stay closed until the sun reappears the next day. This reaction to light, known as photonasty, or sleeping posture, uses the same mechanics as the mimosa's reaction to touch. The reaction to light is, however, somewhat slower. When moved from light to dark a mimosa plant will take about 30 minutes to close. The plant will open again only when light hits the leaf cushions.

Day *(top)* **and night** *(bottom)*

The wood sorrel opens in daylight *(top)* and closes up at night *(bottom)*.

Do Some Plants Eat Insects?

Some plants, called insectivorous plants, have special leaves for catching insects. Although these plants also live by photosynthesis to get their nutrients, they often grow in acidic soils or in water low in the minerals nitrogen, phosphorus, and potassium. Scientists speculate that insectivorous plants must feed on insects to supplement their meager intake of nutrients. The plants use various devious traps including a pot-shaped pitfall, leaves that close like a clamshell, sticky surfaces, and a water-straining method.

Fatal attraction

The Venus's-flytrap, native to the grasslands of North America *(below)*, catches insects by snapping its two leaves shut like a shell when an insect walks on the surface of the leaves.

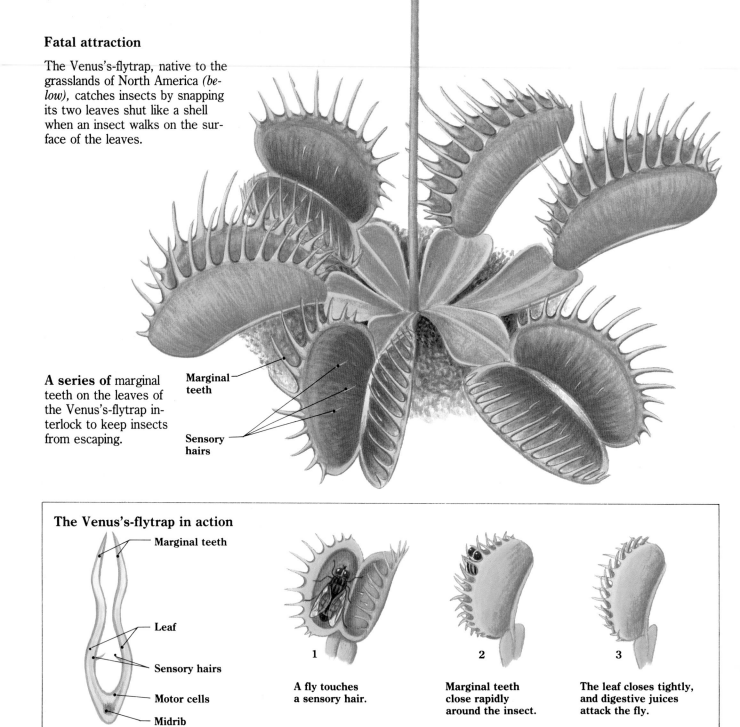

A series of marginal teeth on the leaves of the Venus's-flytrap interlock to keep insects from escaping.

Marginal teeth

Sensory hairs

The Venus's-flytrap in action

Marginal teeth

Leaf

Sensory hairs

Motor cells

Midrib

1
A fly touches a sensory hair.

2
Marginal teeth close rapidly around the insect.

3
The leaf closes tightly, and digestive juices attack the fly.

How a pitfall trap works

The *Nepenthes* pitcher plant *(below)* lures insects with odor and nectar. Once in the jug-shaped insectivorous sac, the insects are unable to escape and eventually decompose in the plant's digestive juices.

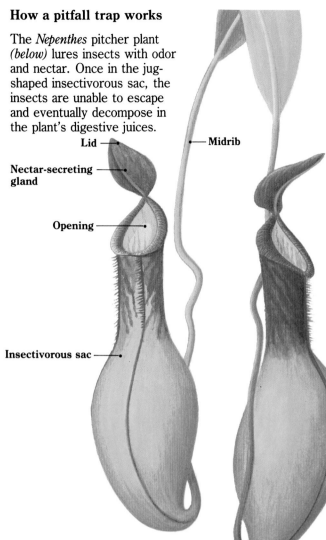

Lid

Nectar-secreting gland

Opening

Insectivorous sac

Midrib

There are 65 varieties of the insectivorous *Nepenthes* pitcher plant in China, Southeast Asia, Sri Lanka, India, Madagascar, and elsewhere. Often found climbing in forests, *Nepenthes* usually catches many ants.

The insectivorous sac

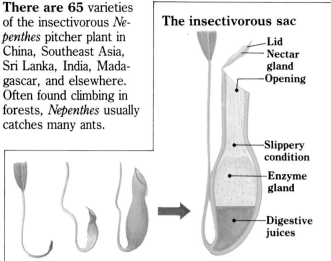

Lid
Nectar gland
Opening

Slippery condition

Enzyme gland

Digestive juices

An insectivorous sac grows from a swelling at the tip of the *Nepenthes* vine. The lid opens as the sac grows.

The tube-shaped leaves of the *Sarracenia* pitcher plant grow in the springtime and attract mostly winged insects. An odor from the tube's interior entices the insects. Once the insects are inside, thick downward-pointing needles keep them entrapped. Scientists suspect that the leaf secretes a narcotic that drugs its prey.

***Sarracenia*'s deadly tube**

Sticky glue

The 85 species of sundew plant that grow throughout the world employ a sticky mucus to trap their prey. This mucus, secreted by the leaf's dense covering of gland hairs, is more than just sticky. It contains the juices that digest the trapped insect. The gland hairs push the trapped insect downward while the leaf blades wrap around it.

Sucking up its victims

The bladderwort *(Utricularia)*, sometimes considered a trapping plant, grows in the streams and wetlands of Japan, China, and Sakhalin Island, Russia. The entrance to its insectivorous sac is controlled by a valve, which opens to take in water rich in protozoa, water fleas, and insect larvae. The sac then expels the water and uses its absorption hairs to digest the creatures.

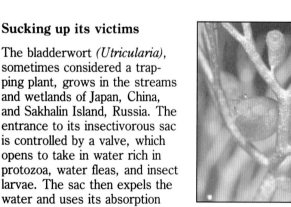

Bladderwort's watery trap

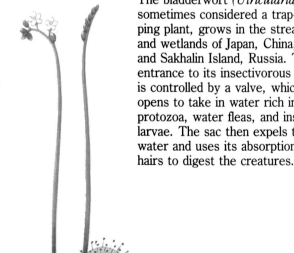

Trapped by a sundew

When microscopic water dwellers touch the thin hairs at the entrance to the bladderwort's sac, a valve opens and water pressure forces the victims into the trap.

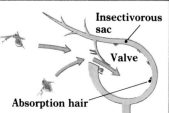

Insectivorous sac

Valve

Absorption hair

Are Pine Needles Really Leaves?

Although they may appear quite different from the flat, wide leaves of other trees, pine needles are leaves nonetheless. Functionally they are no different from other leaves. They have chloroplasts, with which they perform photosynthesis, and use stomas for respiration and transpiration. Structurally, however, pine needles are different. There is, for example, only one vein running through the center of the needle to carry water and nutrients, as opposed to the numerous veins in a flat leaf. Pine needles have a thick epidermis that allows them to survive in any climate from tropical to polar, and a long, sharp, narrow shape that makes it difficult to distinguish the front from the back.

Built for harsh climates

The pine needle, which gets its name from its long, thin shape, is coated with a thick, waxy cuticle that reduces water evaporation. Pine needles are also resistant to freezing, which makes them well suited to cold climates.

Pine needle attachment

Pine branches are divided into long and short lengths. The needles are normally attached at the tip of the short branch in bundles, or fascicles, of two, three, or five.

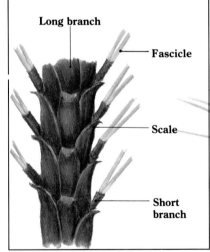

Long branch

Fascicle

Scale

Short branch

An ancient Japanese black pine

Fascicle

Short branch

Long branch

The Japanese black pine, a tall evergreen found in Japan and parts of South Korea, has dark gray bark and hard needles *(above),* with two leaves to a fascicle from 4 to 6 inches in length and about .04 inch wide.

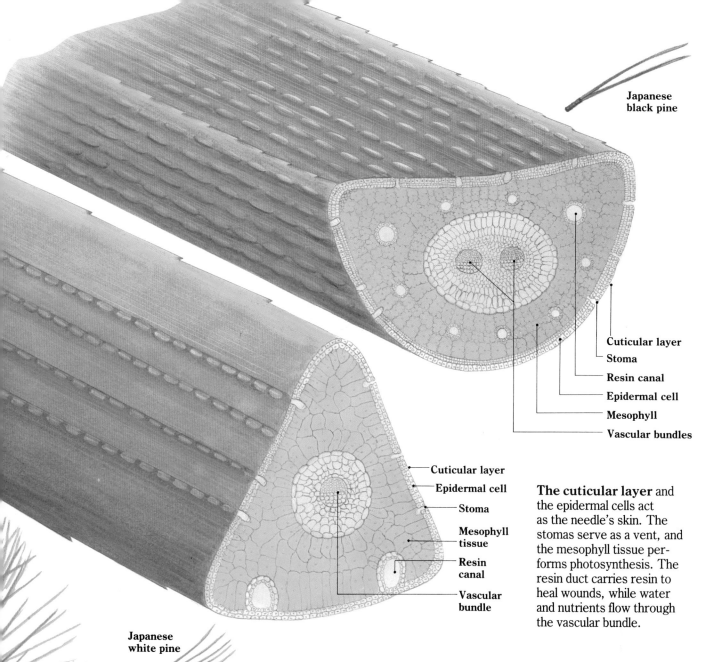

Japanese
black pine

Cuticular layer
Stoma
Resin canal
Epidermal cell
Mesophyll
Vascular bundles

Cuticular layer
Epidermal cell
Stoma
Mesophyll tissue
Resin canal
Vascular bundle

Japanese
white pine

The cuticular layer and the epidermal cells act as the needle's skin. The stomas serve as a vent, and the mesophyll tissue performs photosynthesis. The resin duct carries resin to heal wounds, while water and nutrients flow through the vascular bundle.

The shapes of pine needles

The cross-sectional shape of a pine needle is determined by the number of needles making up a fascicle. The various cross-sectional shapes are categorized as orbicular *(below, left)*, semiorbicular *(below, center)*, and fan-shaped *(below, right)*.

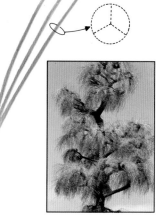

The Japanese red pine is a tall conifer with two needles nearly 5 inches long.

The North American long-leaf pine has three needles that grow to 23 inches.

The five needles of the Japanese white pine grow to about 3.5 inches.

4
Beauty with a Purpose

For humans, flowers have become symbols of fragile, useless beauty. In real, nonsymbolic life, however, flowers are the hardworking and highly successful reproductive tools developed by one large group of plants, called angiosperms.

Flowers vary widely in size, from those of the aquatic *Wolffia,* the size of a sesame seed, to the jungle flower *Rafflesia,* which has the diameter of a washtub. They range in color and beauty from tiny, gray-green grass flowers without petals to large, brightly colored garden flowers and exquisite tropical orchids. Some flowers look like a

child's drawing of a flower: five petals with a round center. Others look like trumpets, pitchers, or even insects.

All these flowers have some structures in common. Male parts, called stamens, consist of a stalk, or filament, and a pollen head, or anther. Female parts, called carpels or pistils, consist of an ovary, where the seed develops, and a stalk, or style, tipped by a sticky stigma, which receives pollen. Stamens and carpels may occur on the same flower, on different flowers of the same plant, or on different plants. To increase variety in their offspring, most plant species avoid pollinating themselves. Instead, flowers rely on a vast variety of pollinating methods, from the wind to insects to bats.

Blooming by day or by night, all around the world, flowers vary from the brilliant azalea *(top left)*, visited here by a swallowtail butterfly, to the giant *Rafflesia (bottom right)*, smelling of carrion and attractive mainly to flies.

Why Do Some Insects Visit Flowers?

Butterflies and bees visit flowers to feed, but they don't harm the plant. Flowering plants and insects—including not only butterflies and bees, but flies, beetles, and others—have formed a close partnership over millions of years of evolution. This partnership helps plants reproduce and feeds the insects.

Plants produce brightly colored flowers with strong odors to attract insects. They also make food in the form of nectar, a thin, nutritious syrup, and extra pollen, tiny, sticky particles that carry the plant's male reproductive cells. But plants also make sure visiting insects carry some pollen intact to the (female) stigma of another plant. By fertilizing different individuals, or cross-pollinating, insects help plants produce more varied offspring. This variety helps the new crop of plants survive different environmental conditions to reproduce again.

In their search for food, insects have evolved long, tubelike mouthparts to reach nectar, as well as special pollen-carrying hairs. Overall, insects pollinate about 80 percent of all flowering plants; but birds, bats and other mammals, and even slugs pollinate some plants.

With their strong sense of smell, butterflies prefer sweet-smelling, colorful flowers like this azalea.

1. The brightly colored corolla attracts insects.

2. A pattern of spots or stripes, called the nectar guide, shows an insect where to find nectar. Some nectar guides reflect only ultraviolet light. People can't see them, but bees can.

3. Deep in the flower lies the nectar gland, or nectary, which makes nectar and scent.

Chemicals color the corolla

Chemicals called pigments give flowers their colors. Some are strong, others mere tints.

1. Colors ranging from baby pink to royal purple come from pigments called anthocyanins.
2. Pigments called carotenoids give carrots their color. They produce colors from lemon yellow to tomato red.
3. Flavones produce the palest yellow tint. Stronger pigments often mask the color of flavones.
4. White flowers have no pigment. Instead, air bubbles in the petals scatter light of all colors.

Different pigments produce the spots or lines of nectar guides. Some reflect ultraviolet light.

Dusting insects with pollen

Some flowers actively place pollen on visiting insects. Using techniques ranging from tapping to trapping, these flowers ensure that no insect leaves without pollen.

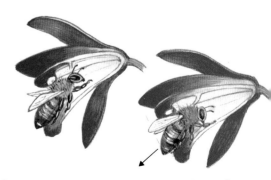

Orchids display the widest variety of pollinating devices. This orchid traps the bee with its stamens. When the bee struggles to escape, it gets smeared with pollen.

Structure of a flower

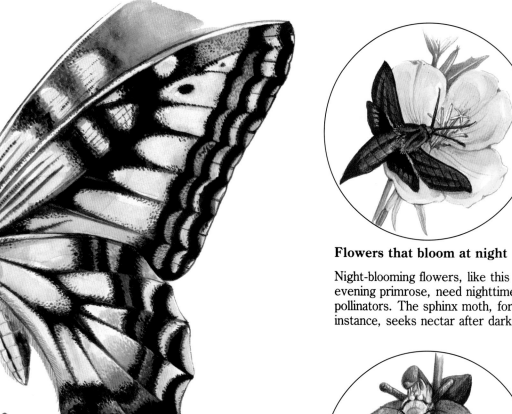

The carpel, or pistil, features a sticky stigma on its tip for catching pollen carried by insects.

Each stamen consists of a long, thin stalk, called a filament, with a pollen-producing anther at the end.

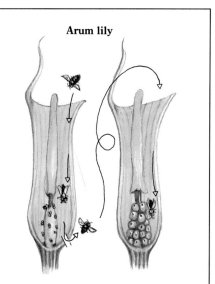

Flowers that bloom at night

Night-blooming flowers, like this evening primrose, need nighttime pollinators. The sphinx moth, for instance, seeks nectar after dark.

A fake female attracts insects

Some orchids look just like a female insect, wings and all. When a male tries to mate, he picks up pollen.

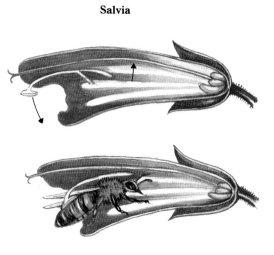

Trefoil

Triggerlike keel

Salvia

Arum lily

In some flowers, two petals form a landing platform called a keel. When an insect lands, the stamens pop up to transfer pollen.

A bee entering a fresh salvia flower triggers the stamens to curl downward, dusting the bee with pollen. The bee then carries the pollen onward.

Some bad-smelling flowers trap flies for long periods of time. When the fly finally makes its escape, it takes pollen to the next flower.

How Do Plants Know When to Bloom?

Some plants bloom in early spring, others in late summer. In addition, many species wait to bloom until the time of year when the length of daylight precisely suits them.

Although plants bloom at different times throughout the warm part of the year, they all fall roughly into three blooming categories. So-called short-day plants bloom late in the summer as nights get longer. Long-day plants bloom in late spring as nights get shorter. Day-neutral plants bloom any time they have enough water and sun to produce flowers.

After these categories were named, scientists discovered that plants don't measure day length. Instead, they count the hours of continuous darkness. Each species may need a different number of nights of the right length. The short-day plant called cocklebur, for example, blooms after a single dark night. Soybeans, on the other hand, need four proper nights in a row. At the opposite extreme from cocklebur is spinach, which must count two weeks of shorter nights.

Day length and blooming

Each species of short-day or long-day plant waits to bloom until one or more nights last a certain number of hours. Poinsettias are short-day plants that need at least 12 hours of darkness to bloom. Spinach, a long-day plant, needs dark periods less than 11 hours long.

Plants can measure the period of darkness precisely. Thirty minutes can make the difference between a night that lasts long enough and one that is too short. And the darkness must not be interrupted. Some species are so sensitive that even a minute of light in the middle of the night can reset the plant's clock and prevent it from blooming.

When flowers open

Some flowers, such as the morning glory (bottom), open at dawn and close before dusk. Tobacco, by contrast, opens only at night. By growing faster on one side than the other, each petal bends, closing or opening the flower.

Cosmos (above), a member of the chrysanthemum family, grows in Mexico.

The soybean, a short-day plant, belongs to the legume family, which includes peas as well as other beans.

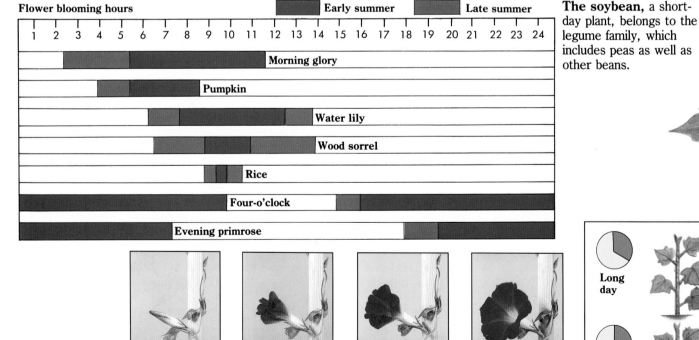

| Flower blooming hours | Early summer | Late summer |
| 1 2 3 4 5 6 7 8 9 10 11 12 13 14 15 16 17 18 19 20 21 22 23 24 |

Morning glory

Pumpkin

Water lily

Wood sorrel

Rice

Four-o'clock

Evening primrose

2:00 a.m.   3:30 a.m.   4:00 a.m.   5:00 a.m.

Long day

Short day

Short-day and long-day plants

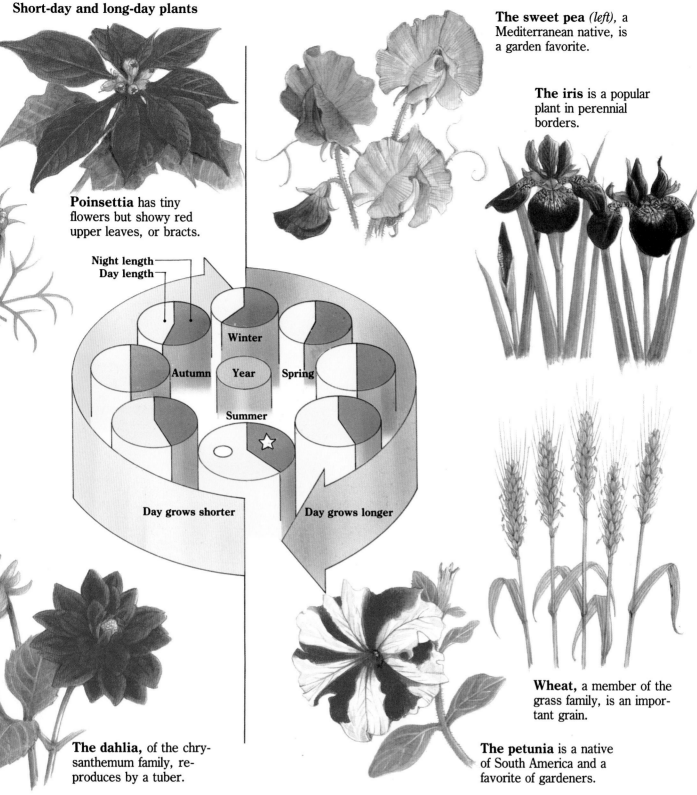

Poinsettia has tiny flowers but showy red upper leaves, or bracts.

The sweet pea *(left),* a Mediterranean native, is a garden favorite.

The iris is a popular plant in perennial borders.

Night length
Day length

Winter

Autumn   Year   Spring

Summer

Day grows shorter

Day grows longer

The dahlia, of the chrysanthemum family, reproduces by a tuber.

Wheat, a member of the grass family, is an important grain.

The petunia is a native of South America and a favorite of gardeners.

The short-day plant called cocklebur, or *Xanthium,* needs a night longer than nine hours to produce flower buds. If only one leaf is covered with black paper, simulating night, the whole plant begins to bloom.

Leaves measure the night

A plant without leaves will never bloom. But if a single leaf is exposed to the correct night length, then grafted to the leafless plant, it can trigger blooming in its new plant. This works even if the donor and recipient are of different species or in different blooming categories. Scientists guess that a chemical must flow from the leaf to the rest of the plant. But after 50 years of searching for this "flowering hormone," they still have not isolated it.

How Big Can Flowers Grow?

The immense flower of the Southeast Asian plant *Rafflesia arnoldii* is one of the most remarkable specimens in the plant world. Growing to the size of a washtub—up to 3 feet across—it can weigh as much as 15 pounds.

Although it produces the world's largest single flower, *Rafflesia* has tiny stems and roots. The plant doesn't need large stems because it grows right on the forest floor. And it doesn't need large roots because it is a parasite, getting its nutrition and water from the stems and roots of other plants.

The purplish red *Rafflesia* flower smells like rotting meat, attracting hundreds of flies. As the flies crawl around in the central bowl, they acci-dentally collect pollen which they carry from flower to flower, pollinating the plants. Once pollinated, the *Rafflesia* flower matures into a large, soft, sticky fruit. In some areas, Asian elephants and other large animals distribute *Rafflesia*'s small, hard seeds in an unusual way. When an elephant steps on a fruit, the seeds stick to its foot and eventually get trampled into the soil near the roots of vines *Rafflesia* parasitizes.

A germinating *Rafflesia* seed sends roots right inside the stems and roots of vines that grow along the ground. Soon a golf-ball-size bud emerges. It slowly grows into a larger bud looking like a brownish cabbage, and after about a year and a half it blooms.

A genus of parasites

Fifty species of the genus *Rafflesia* live in Southeast Asian jungles. *Rafflesia arnoldii,* named after an English botanist, lives only on Sumatra. Its five huge, leathery petals surround a bowl-shaped structure in the center of the flower. Large spikes line the bottom of the bowl. Small stamens and pistils are arranged below the spikes. Most of the tissues of the plant—other than the flower—remain inside the roots and stems of its host.

The *Rafflesia* flower

Inside the central bowl of a *Rafflesia* flower lies a flat, spiky plate that smells like rotting meat. Flies lighting inside the bowl slip to the bottom, where they crawl past the small stamens and pistils.

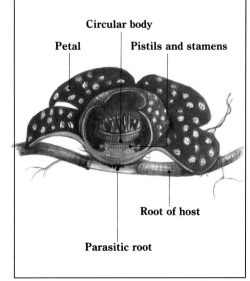

Circular body

Petal

Pistils and stamens

Root of host

Parasitic root

Other parasitic plants

All plants need water, minerals, and food. Most green plants absorb water and minerals from the soil through their roots. They make food from carbon dioxide and water using the sun's energy and a green pigment called chlorophyll. Completely parasitic plants such as *Rafflesia* get all three necessities from host plants. *Rafflesia* and other parasites have no leaves and therefore no chlorophyll.

Partially parasitic plants, such as mistletoe, have green leaves and make some of their own food, so they mainly take only water and minerals from their host. Other plants absorb nutrients from decaying matter in the forest soil. These are not parasites but saprophytes.

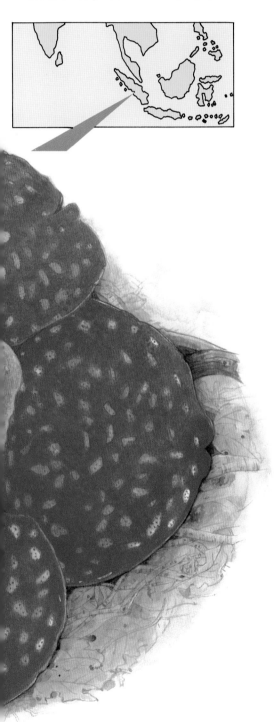

Broomrape and members of its family parasitize leafy plants such as grasses.

This form of broomrape lacks chlorophyll and taps into the roots of leafy plants.

Dodder, a kind of morning glory, climbs plants, sucking nutrients from the stems.

Climbing parasites send a root into the stems of the host to get nutrients.

The figwort makes its own food. But it gets minerals and water from host plants.

This member of the sandalwood family parasitizes plants for minerals and water.

57

Do Flowers Have Different Sexes?

Flowers in most plant species contain both male stamens and female carpels. But some species have evolved separate sexes. In such plants, all the flowers on an individual plant are male (with stamens) or female (with one or more carpels). These plants cannot self-pollinate.

When flowers with both sexes self-pollinate, they produce offspring that are exactly the same as the parent plant. If environmental conditions should suddenly change, however, a population of identical plants could die out. A varied population, on the other hand, might contain some individuals that could survive. So a species gains an advantage by avoiding self-pollination.

In addition to completely separate sexes, plants have evolved other means to avoid self-pollination. In some species, each flower may carry either stamens or carpels, but not both. Although this reduces the chance of self-pollination, some plants take the extra step of making sure that male flowers do not mature at the same time as female flowers. Even flowers with both stamens and pistils can avoid self-pollination. Often the stamens will mature first. They shed their pollen and wither before the carpel matures. Later, the mature carpel develops a sticky stigma to receive pollen carried by insects from a different plant.

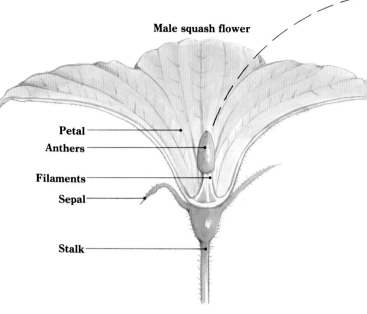

Male squash flower

Squash flowers have five large yellow petals with five smaller green sepals underneath. The five stamens with the pollen-bearing anthers on the end are bundled together in the center like a single structure.

Petal
Anthers
Filaments
Sepal
Stalk

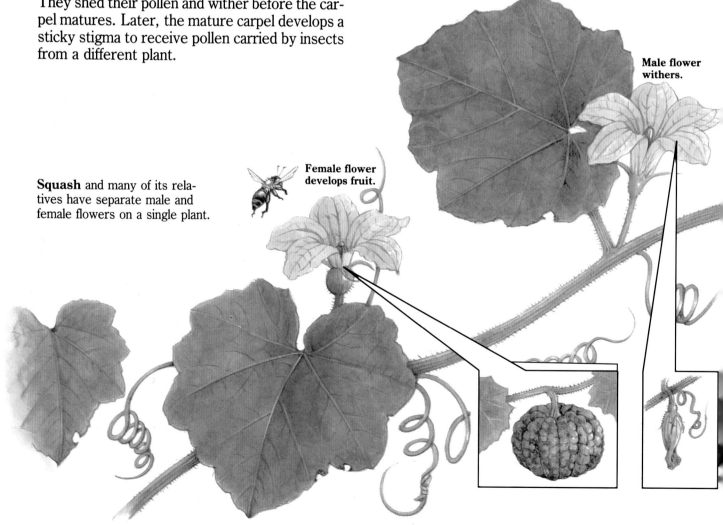

Male flower withers.

Female flower develops fruit.

Squash and many of its relatives have separate male and female flowers on a single plant.

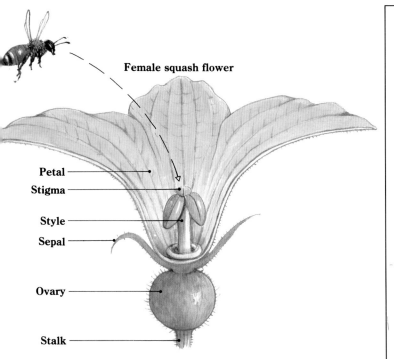

Female squash flower

Petal
Stigma
Style
Sepal
Ovary
Stalk

Female squash flower

A female squash flower looks much like the male flower. The female structure, or carpel, consists of an ovary below the five petals and five sepals, and a stalk, or style, topped by a three-part stigma for receiving pollen.

Variety versus volume

By avoiding self-pollination, plants gain the advantage of variety in their offspring. But, at the same time, by doing this they reduce the number of seeds they produce.

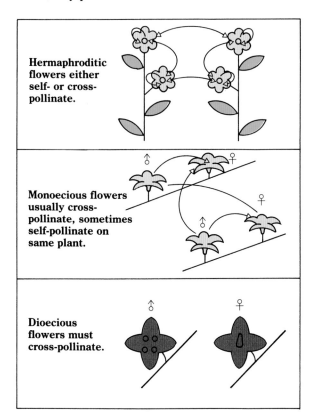

Hermaphroditic flowers either self- or cross-pollinate.

Monoecious flowers usually cross-pollinate, sometimes self-pollinate on same plant.

Dioecious flowers must cross-pollinate.

Plant techniques

Plants in which each flower has both stamens and carpels are called hermaphroditic. Those with separate male and female flowers are called monoecious. And those in which each individual is either male or female are called dioecious.

Male and female flowers on a single plant may be separated like those of the chestnut *(below, left),* which has a few female flowers at the base of the flower stalk and many male flowers nearer the tip. Or they may look different, like the *Akebia's* flowers *(below, right).* This difference in appearance discourages insects from flitting from a male to a female flower on the same plant.

The chestnut and *Akebia* plants have different ways of avoiding self-pollination.

The flowers of dioecious plants may have widely differing appearances. The male cycad flower, or cone *(below, left),* for instance, reaches a length of 3 feet, whereas the female cone *(right)* is short and wide.

Cycad flowers: male *(left),* female *(right).*

In hermaphroditic flowers, the stamens may mature before the carpel, or the carpel may mature before the stamens. Either sequence prevents self-pollination. In the bellflower *(below),* the stamen matures, sheds pollen, and dries out before the stigma spreads to receive pollen.

The stamens in the bellflower mature first *(left).* Later, the carpel matures *(right).*

59

How Do Tulips Open and Close?

Some flowers, such as the tulip, open every morning and close every night. Each evening, tulip petals bend upward and the flower closes. Every morning the flower opens again.

Surprisingly, the petals are reacting not to changes in light but to changes in temperature. When the temperature drops as evening comes on, the cells on the outer surface of each petal grow slightly faster than the cells on the inner surface. This growth forces the petal to curve inward. In the morning, as the temperature begins to rise, the cells on the inside of each petal begin growing faster, forcing the petal into a straighter shape and opening the flower. The tulip will also open if it is moved from a cold room into a warm one, even if the light is the same in each room.

Other flowers open and close in response to light and dark. And some have a sort of internal clock. They will open and close every 12 hours even if the light or temperature never changes.

A tulip opens and closes

On a cool morning, the cells on both sides of the tulip petal grow at the same speed.

The tulip came originally from central Asia but now grows in gardens the world over. The Netherlands exports many tulip bulbs, which are planted in the autumn.

How flowers open and close

As middle-distance runners know, the distance around the outside of a curve is longer than that around the inside. When cells on one side of a petal lengthen, the petal curves in the opposite direction.

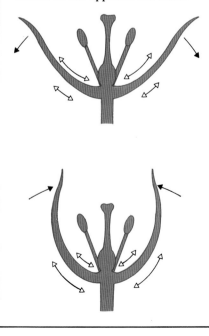

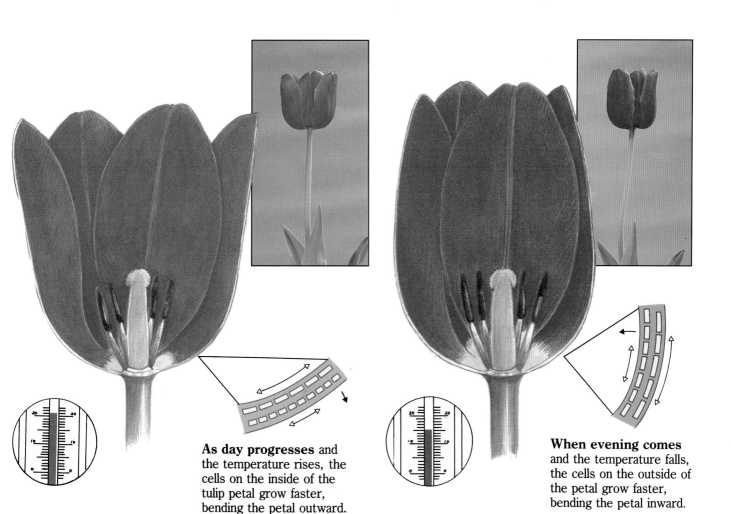

As day progresses and the temperature rises, the cells on the inside of the tulip petal grow faster, bending the petal outward.

When evening comes and the temperature falls, the cells on the outside of the petal grow faster, bending the petal inward.

Responding to light

Many flowers open and close in response to light. Scientists think flowers may open at times when pollinating insects are most likely to be active. Gentians and marigolds open at dawn and close at dusk. Tobacco flowers, on the other hand, open in the evening. A cloudy, dark day prevents day-opening flowers from responding. In some cases, a flower will continue to open and close even when kept in the dark.

Gentian opening and closing

In the gentian, only part of the petal moves. The cells grow faster on the outside surface to close and twist the petal tips.

About 500 species of gentian flourish worldwide. Some species live high in mountains, while close relatives live in arctic regions.

A gentian opens in light *(left)* and twists to close in darkness *(right)*.

Do Grass Plants Have Flowers?

Tiny grass flowers, lacking petals and sepals, may be hard to see, but grasses reproduce much as do other flowering plants. Instead of attracting insects with colorful petals, grasses rely on wind for pollination. Although many kinds of grasses can spread without producing seeds, sexual reproduction has allowed the grass family to evolve into a large, successful group.

Grass flowers grow three long stamens and a single carpel with two stigmas. Most grasses ensure cross-pollination by developing the stamens first and the stigmas later. Some species have separate male and female flowers on a single plant. Separate male and female plants are rare in the grass family.

Grass fruits, called grain, supply food for nearly every human in the world. Wheat, oats, barley, rice, corn, and sugarcane all belong to the grass family. People cultivate cereal grasses not only for food but also to feed livestock.

Structure of a grass flower

Grass flowers sprout from the end of the stem in groups called spikelets, having up to 20 flowers each. Each individual flower has only one ovary and grows a single seed, or grain.

Arista

Stigma

Anther

Secondary glume

Grass flower

The spike contains several spikelets, each with several flowers.

Lawn grass spreads in two ways. It makes flowers and seeds as other flowering plants do. But it can also spread by way of underground stems that sprout new plants every few inches.

The parts of a grass plant

Several leaflike sheaths wrap around a grass flower. Inside lie three stamens, each with a filament and an anther, and a carpel with an ovary and two stigmas.

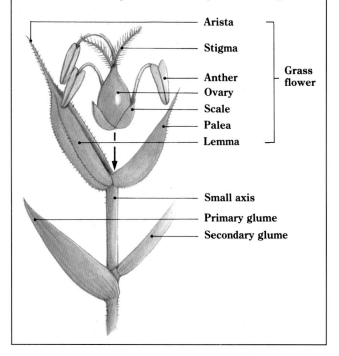

Arista

Stigma

Anther

Ovary — Grass flower

Scale

Palea

Lemma

Small axis

Primary glume

Secondary glume

Varieties of lawn grass

A wide variety of grasses are used for lawns. Some species tolerate shade well, others tolerate rough use. Grass seed intended for home lawns often contains a mixture of species. Because of their fast seed production and growth by underground stems, grasses can quickly cover newly disturbed soil. Although stamens and stigmas mature at different times in many grasses, the illustrations here show both in the mature condition.

Bermuda grass

Bent grass

Kentucky bluegrass

Red fescue

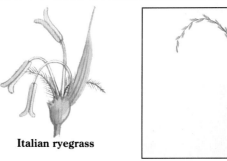

Italian ryegrass

Filament of stamen
Flowering glume
Ovary
Flower stem
Secondary axis

Lawn grass blooms.

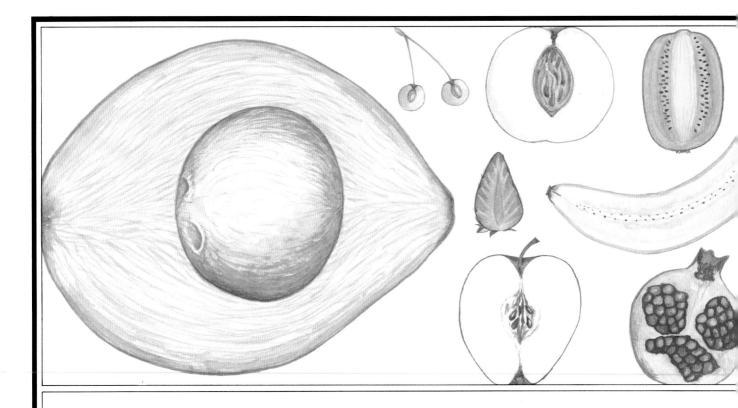

5

Fruits and Seeds

Like most living things, plants must bring male and female cells together to reproduce their kind. But plants have a special problem after their eggs are fertilized: How can they spread their seeds? Because plants cannot move from place to place, they have evolved various methods for dispersing their progeny. Some seeds just drop to the ground. Others sail through the air on tiny parachutes or wings. Others float on ocean waves. But the most remarkable methods

are the partnerships that have evolved between plants and animals to take seeds to new ground.

To attract birds and mammals, many plants grow nutritious, often colorful or fragrant fruits around their seeds. When animals eat the fruit, they accidentally carry seeds from place to place. Sometimes the animals swallow the seeds and later deposit them along with droppings. Other times, the seeds stick to beaks, feathers, or fur, only to fall off later, far from the parent plant.

Many seeds—we call them nuts—contain nutritious substances right in the seed. Animals eat some and hide others for later consumption. Those they don't eat may sprout, creating new plants and beginning the cycle again.

Fruits come in a colorful variety of shapes and sizes, from stone fruits such as cherries and peaches to multiple fruits such as pineapples *(shown below and in the cutaway above)*.

How Do Flowers Make Fruit?

After pollination, a flower starts to change dramatically. Many parts of the flower may grow, depending on the species. This growth results in the foods we call fruits, nuts, grains, and in some cases vegetables. Plants make sweet fruits to attract birds and bats just as they make colorful flowers to attract insects. When an animal eats the fruit, it accidentally scatters the seeds. In this way, the plant species spreads.

Seed growth begins when a pollen grain lands on the sticky stigma at the tip of the carpel, the female structure. The pollen grain contains two sperm, or male reproductive cells. A tube grows down from the stigma through the style to the ovary. There, one sperm fuses with the egg cell, or ovum. This cell becomes the embryo. The other sperm fuses with two other cells, becoming a tissue called endosperm, which nourishes the embryo. The starchy, nutritious part of grains such as wheat and oats comes from endosperm.

Simple fruits: ovaries alone

A fruit that grows from an ovary consists of three layers surrounding the seed: a skin; a thick, fleshy middle layer; and a tough or hard inner layer. All three layers make up the pericarp. Simple fruits grow from one or more ovaries.

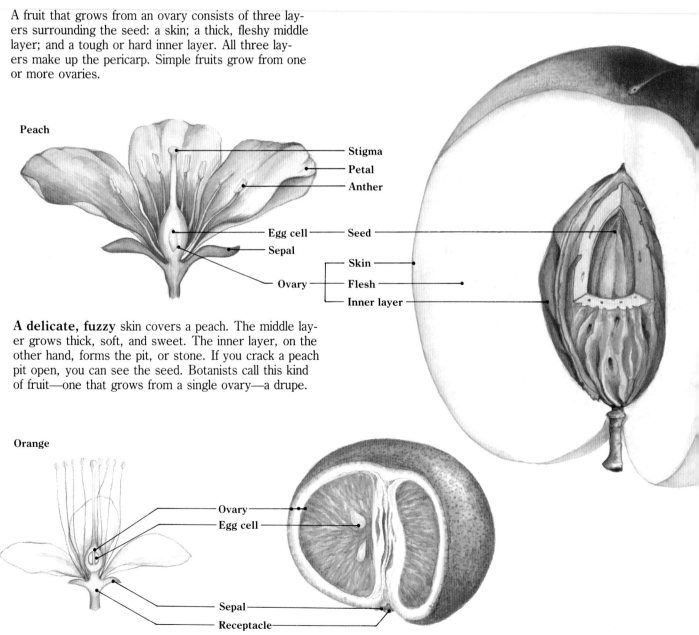

Peach

- Stigma
- Petal
- Anther
- Egg cell — Seed
- Sepal
- Ovary — Skin
- Flesh
- Inner layer

A delicate, fuzzy skin covers a peach. The middle layer grows thick, soft, and sweet. The inner layer, on the other hand, forms the pit, or stone. If you crack a peach pit open, you can see the seed. Botanists call this kind of fruit—one that grows from a single ovary—a drupe.

Orange

- Ovary
- Egg cell
- Sepal
- Receptacle

Berries grow from several ovaries fused together. In the orange, a type of berry, the skin is thick and leathery, and the inner layer divides the flesh into segments.

Complex fruits

Complex fruits grow from many separate ovaries, and sometimes from tissues other than the ovary. In some plants, such as the raspberry, a single flower produces a fruit from many ovaries (and therefore with many seeds) called an aggregate fruit. In others, many flowers fuse to produce a fruit called a multiple fruit.

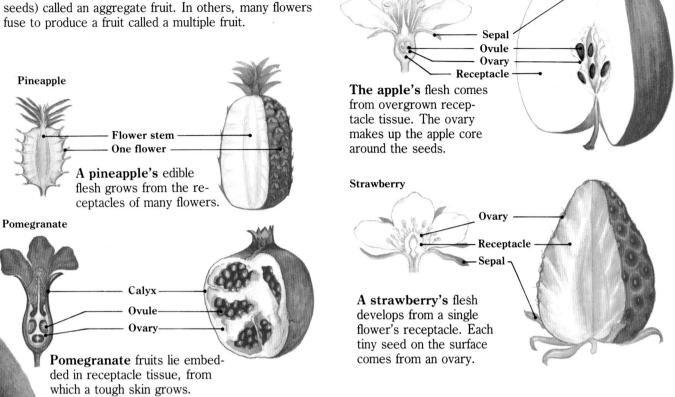

Apple

Sepal
Ovule
Ovary
Receptacle

The apple's flesh comes from overgrown receptacle tissue. The ovary makes up the apple core around the seeds.

Pineapple

Flower stem
One flower

A pineapple's edible flesh grows from the receptacles of many flowers.

Pomegranate

Calyx
Ovule
Ovary

Pomegranate fruits lie embedded in receptacle tissue, from which a tough skin grows.

Strawberry

Ovary
Receptacle
Sepal

A strawberry's flesh develops from a single flower's receptacle. Each tiny seed on the surface comes from an ovary.

A variety of fruits

Pollinated flowers develop in a variety of ways, producing fruits, grains, beans, and nuts. Simple fruits, which come from a single ovary, may grow delicious juicy layers, or they may be dry. Aggregate fruits, which grow from many ovaries in a single flower, may develop juicy flesh from the receptacle or from the ovaries, as in the raspberry. Multiple fruits grow from many flowers fused together.

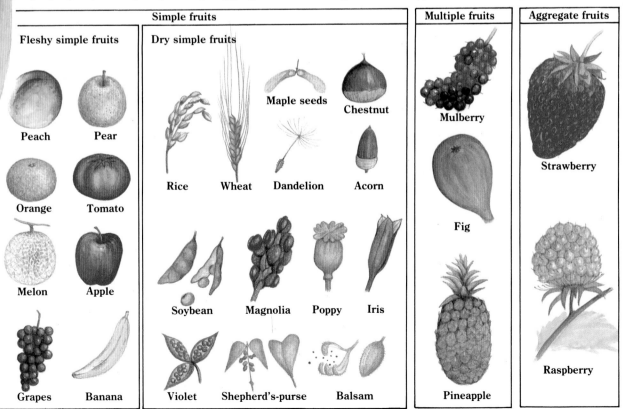

Simple fruits		Multiple fruits	Aggregate fruits
Fleshy simple fruits	**Dry simple fruits**		

Fleshy simple fruits: Peach, Pear, Orange, Tomato, Melon, Apple, Grapes, Banana

Dry simple fruits: Maple seeds, Chestnut, Rice, Wheat, Dandelion, Acorn, Soybean, Magnolia, Poppy, Iris, Violet, Shepherd's-purse, Balsam

Multiple fruits: Mulberry, Fig, Pineapple

Aggregate fruits: Strawberry, Raspberry

Can Figs Grow without Flowers?

Without a close look, one might think figs grow fruits without flowers. But the fig flowers are just hidden inside the fruit. The sweet flesh of a fig actually consists of a swollen stem, or receptacle, growing around a cluster of flowers. The stem grows in the shape of a vase, and the flowers sprout inside the vase. Only a small opening remains in the end of the fruit.

Wild figs grow three kinds of flowers in each fruit: male flowers, female flowers, and gall flowers, which do not form seeds. Specialized wasps, known as fig wasps, pollinate figs, laying eggs in the gall flowers.

Cultivated figs may have only female flowers. Some varieties can develop fruit without being pollinated, but usually wasps carry pollen from male flowers of another tree. Fig farmers sometimes graft on a branch from a variety with male flowers to encourage wasps to pollinate the fruit-bearing trees.

The fig tree

About 800 species of fig trees, belonging to the mulberry family, grow in tropical regions. Besides fruit-producing trees, the fig genus *Ficus* includes the strangler fig, the banyan tree, and the rubber plant.

The sweet inner pulp of a fig grows from the ovaries of many fig flowers. Each will produce a tiny seed.

The outer flesh of a fig develops from the swollen stem, or receptacle, of the flower cluster.

Fig fruit

Flower clusters become fruit

In both fig and pineapple plants, large clusters of flowers, or inflorescences, grow into the fruit people eat. But they grow in opposite ways. As a fig receptacle grows it wraps around the flowers, turning the whole cluster inside out.

Both the receptacle and the individual fruits can be eaten. The receptacle of a pineapple grows with the flowers still on the outside. The pineapple's stem becomes the core, and many flowers form the fruity flesh and the skin.

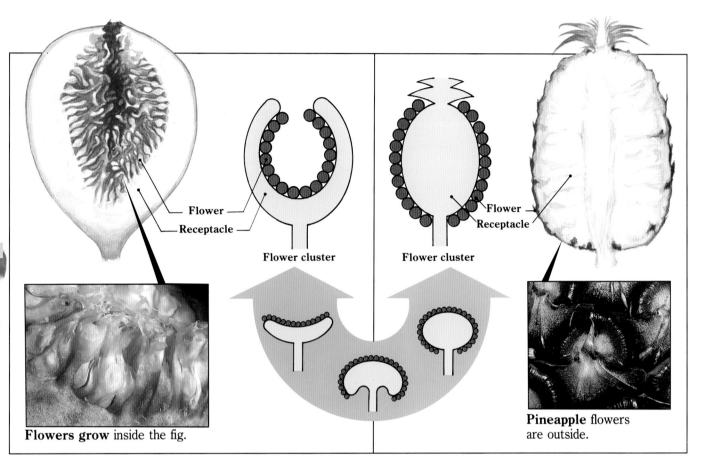

Flower

Receptacle

Flower cluster

Flower cluster

Flower
Receptacle

Flowers grow inside the fig.

Pineapple flowers are outside.

Fig pollination

In wild figs, male flowers grow near the opening, and both female and gall flowers grow near the bottom, inside the fruit. A female fig wasp lays eggs in the gall flowers. When the eggs hatch, the grubs feed on the gall flowers. As the male and female wasps mature, they remain inside the fig to mate. The blind, wingless males die after mating, but the females crawl out. As they leave, they pass male flowers near the opening, collecting pollen in pollen baskets. Each fig-wasp species can only reproduce in a single species of fig, and that fig species relies on its own wasp for pollination.

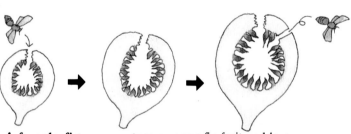

A female fig wasp enters a young fig fruit and lays eggs. The eggs hatch, and the wasps mate inside the fig. Later, a fertilized female flies out, carrying pollen to another fig plant.

Flowers that self-pollinate

Some plants, such as the violet shown here, produce self-pollinating flowers at certain times of the year. In the spring, insects cross-pollinate violet flowers. But in the cooler autumn, another crop of flowers grows. These never open. Instead, pollen from the stamens falls directly onto the stigmas of the same flower, producing a second set of seeds.

The offspring produced by such self-pollination contain a mixture of genes from the parent plant. Although they are not identical to the parent, they do not have the variety produced by cross-pollination.

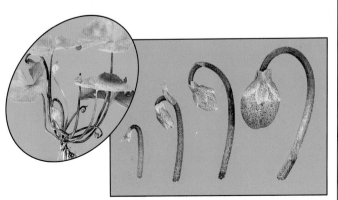

A self-pollinating violet grows fruit.

Why Do Sunflowers Make Many Seeds?

A garden sunflower looks like one gigantic flower, but it actually consists of many hundreds of tiny flowers. These tiny flowers all crowd together in a flower head, or inflorescence. The petals around the edge of the sunflower each belong to a single flower. These flowers do not make seeds. In the center, smaller, tubular flowers each make a fruit with one seed. What we call sunflower seeds are actually dry fruits with a hard skin, or outer pericarp.

Many other familiar flowers, such as daisies, dandelions, and thistles, belong to the sunflower family. Because they all have flower heads composed of many tiny, stalkless flowers, botanists call the family the Compositae.

The garden sunflower

A native of North America, or possibly Peru, the garden sunflower was cultivated before AD 1000 in the southwestern part of the United States. Wild plants have flower heads 6 inches across, but cultivated varieties grow 15 feet high, with heads 2 feet wide.

In addition to cultivating sunflowers for snacks and birdseed, farmers in some parts of the world produce sunflower oil for use in cooking and soap making.

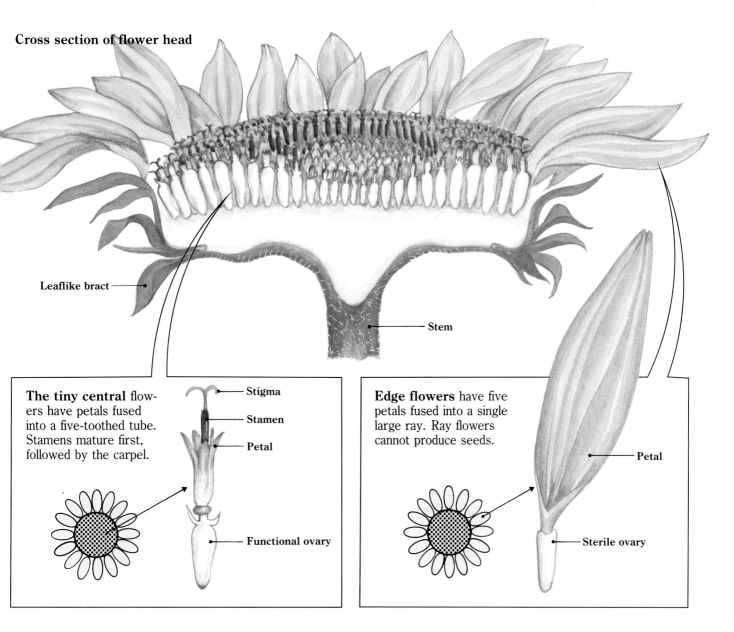

Cross section of flower head

Leaflike bract

Stem

The tiny central flowers have petals fused into a five-toothed tube. Stamens mature first, followed by the carpel.

Stigma

Stamen

Petal

Functional ovary

Edge flowers have five petals fused into a single large ray. Ray flowers cannot produce seeds.

Petal

Sterile ovary

How sunflowers bloom

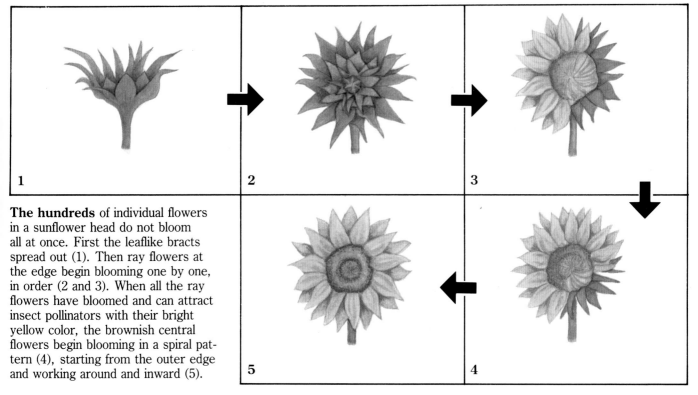

1

2

3

5

4

The hundreds of individual flowers in a sunflower head do not bloom all at once. First the leaflike bracts spread out (1). Then ray flowers at the edge begin blooming one by one, in order (2 and 3). When all the ray flowers have bloomed and can attract insect pollinators with their bright yellow color, the brownish central flowers begin blooming in a spiral pattern (4), starting from the outer edge and working around and inward (5).

What Makes Dandelion Seeds Fly?

The tiny flying parasols we call dandelion seeds are actually fruits. The feathery hairs that make up the parasol grow at the base of the flower, just above the ovary. In fact, the dandelion consists of a large number of tiny flowers, each with five petals fused into a single straplike petal. After a flower is pollinated, this petal falls off, and a thin stalk grows between the hairs and the dry fruit produced by the ovary. A puff of wind sets the seed sailing. The large surface area of the circle of hairs catches the wind, carrying the seed far from the parent plant.

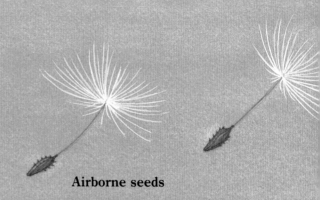

Airborne seeds

When the fruit is fully mature, a puff of wind pulls it away from the seed head, and wind pressure on the light circle of hairs, called a pappus, lifts the fruit through the air. The fruit hangs from its pappus until it settles to the ground. Then the pappus breaks off and the seed sinks into the ground, aided by tiny spines.

The dandelion flower

Like other members of the sunflower family, a dandelion flower head contains hundreds of tiny flowers. Rings of over-lapping leaflike bracts protect the flower head as the fruits mature.

Dandelion flower

Dandelion plant

Fruits carried by the wind

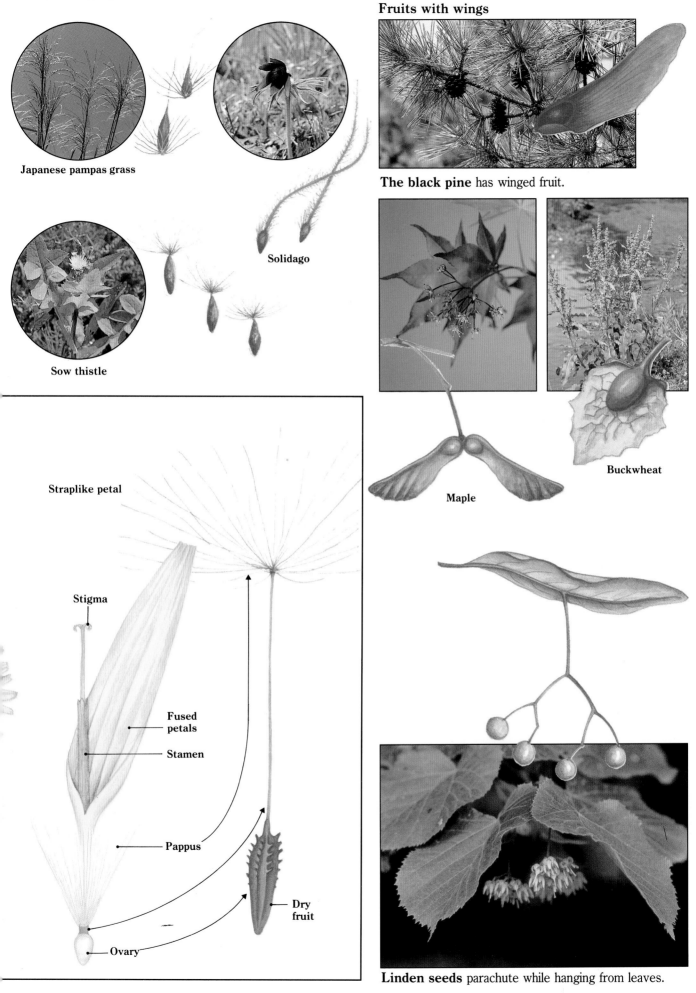

Japanese pampas grass

Solidago

Sow thistle

Fruits with wings

The black pine has winged fruit.

Straplike petal

Stigma

Fused petals

Stamen

Pappus

Ovary

Dry fruit

Maple

Buckwheat

Linden seeds parachute while hanging from leaves.

How Can Bur Marigolds Spread?

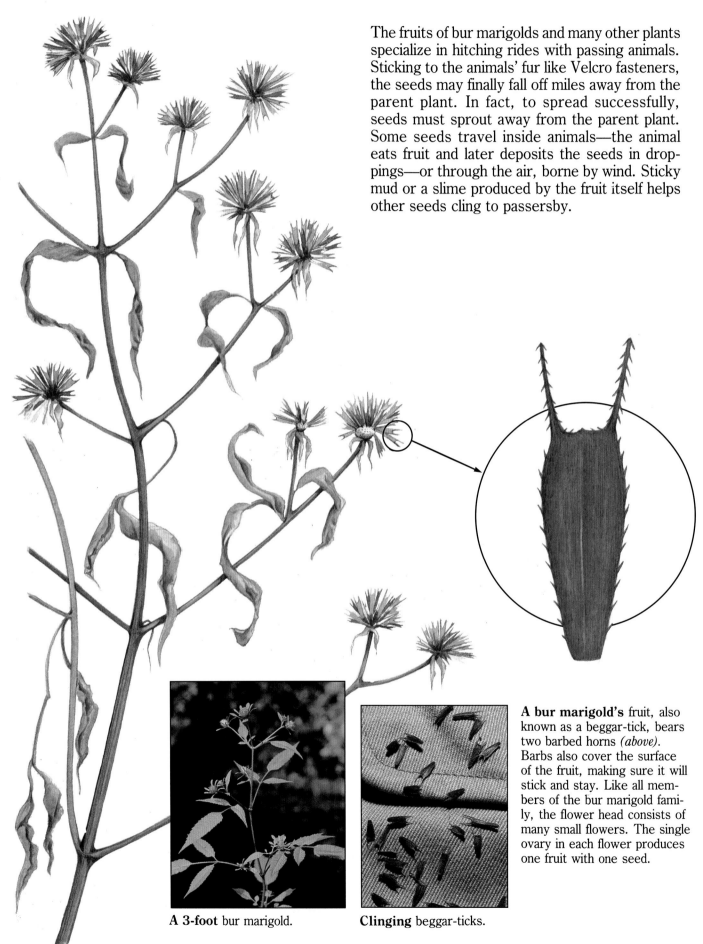

The fruits of bur marigolds and many other plants specialize in hitching rides with passing animals. Sticking to the animals' fur like Velcro fasteners, the seeds may finally fall off miles away from the parent plant. In fact, to spread successfully, seeds must sprout away from the parent plant. Some seeds travel inside animals—the animal eats fruit and later deposits the seeds in droppings—or through the air, borne by wind. Sticky mud or a slime produced by the fruit itself helps other seeds cling to passersby.

A bur marigold's fruit, also known as a beggar-tick, bears two barbed horns *(above)*. Barbs also cover the surface of the fruit, making sure it will stick and stay. Like all members of the bur marigold family, the flower head consists of many small flowers. The single ovary in each flower produces one fruit with one seed.

A 3-foot bur marigold.

Clinging beggar-ticks.

Seeds carried by animals

Seeds can stick to the outside of animals in a variety of ways. Water birds can carry seeds in mud stuck to their feet. Other seeds use hooks or barbs to cling to furry coats, or stick with a gluelike slime.

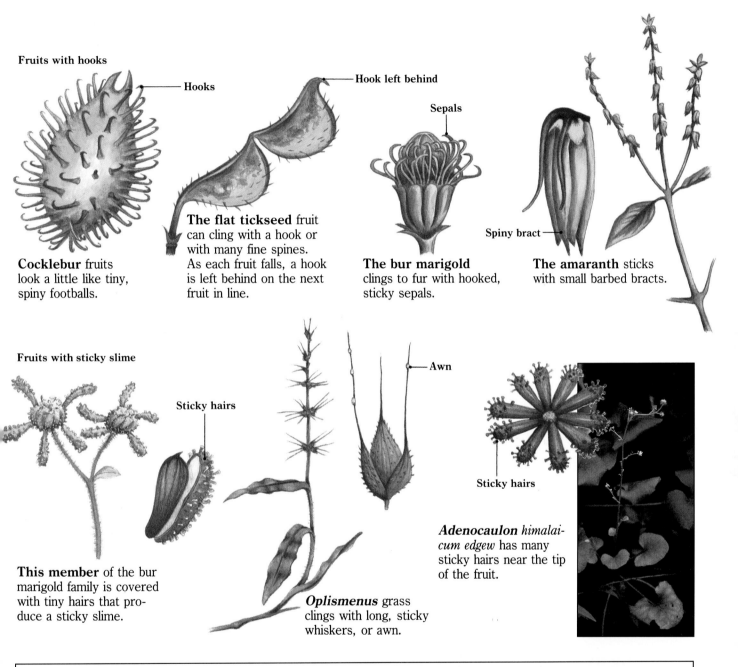

Fruits with hooks

Hooks

Cocklebur fruits look a little like tiny, spiny footballs.

Hook left behind

The flat tickseed fruit can cling with a hook or with many fine spines. As each fruit falls, a hook is left behind on the next fruit in line.

Sepals

The bur marigold clings to fur with hooked, sticky sepals.

Spiny bract

The amaranth sticks with small barbed bracts.

Fruits with sticky slime

Sticky hairs

This member of the bur marigold family is covered with tiny hairs that produce a sticky slime.

Awn

Oplismenus grass clings with long, sticky whiskers, or awn.

Sticky hairs

Adenocaulon *himalaicum edgew* has many sticky hairs near the tip of the fruit.

Naturalized plants

People have carried plants around the world both accidentally and on purpose. In fact, most cultivated plants and most weeds in the United States come from afar. If a plant thrives in its new home, we say that it is naturalized. But success for the plant may spell danger for native ecosystems. Some oversuccessful plants include the pigweed, naturalized in Japan from North America, and the kudzu vine, brought to North America from Japan.

Pigweed

Kudzu vine

Why Do Some Fruits Pop Open?

The fruits of some plants spread their seeds by popping open suddenly. When the fruit pops, the seeds go flying. Fruits can pop for a variety of reasons. Some develop tension as they grow, like a spring that is slowly coiled. Others dry in such a way that the pod pops suddenly to spit the seeds out. In some fleshy fruits, water pressure builds up inside until the skin splits, spraying pulp and seeds far and wide. The fruits called nuts often just fall to the ground. But being round and smooth, they may roll some distance. Squirrels carry some nuts to hiding places, where the seeds can later sprout.

In an impatiens fruit, the inside surface of each carpel grows more slowly than the outside surface. When it is mature, the slightest touch splits the fruit as the carpels suddenly curl up.

Impatiens

The impatiens is a small plant that grows in damp woods. Its complex flowers develop into five-sided fruits.

The five carpels of the impatiens fruit *(above)* have sprung apart, each curling and flinging seeds.

More popping fruits

Some fruits pop because their inside and outside surfaces grow at different rates. Others pop because the inside and the outside of the mature fruit dry differently. Sometimes dry fruits will swell in the rain or moist weather. Some even build up so much water pressure inside that they explode like water balloons.

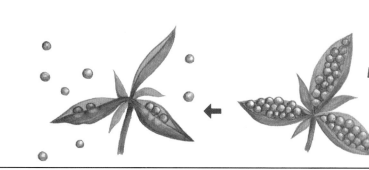

Violet

As the violet seed pod dries, the sides squeeze together, squirting out the seeds.

Wood sorrel

When seed coats shrink, slimy seeds suddenly pop out.

Cranesbill

Thin threads dry and suddenly curl upward, catapulting seeds away.

Impatiens

A mere touch causes carpels to curl suddenly. The whole seed pod flies through the air, scattering seeds.

Squirting cucumber

Water pressure builds inside a mature fruit. Suddenly seeds spray out in a high-pressure jet of sloppy pulp.

Fruits that fall and roll

Heavy, round, and smooth, the fruits we call nuts merely fall to the ground, where they may roll a short distance from the tree. These plants seem to use only the most primitive force for seed scattering—gravity. But nut trees also use animals to spread their wealth. They produce large numbers of fruits at once, too many for squirrels to eat. The squirrels hoard the nuts for winter, placing some in holes in trees and burying others. A few of the buried nuts survive the winter to sprout the next spring.

Evergreen oak

Chestnut

Oak

Japanese oak

Beech

Why Are Fruits and Nuts Colored?

When a bird lands on a branch to peck a bright berry, it is attracted by the color. Birds see red easily but don't have a good sense of smell, so fruits spread by birds are bright but not fragrant. After eating the sweet, ripe fruit, the bird flies away. Later the bird will deposit the seeds in its droppings far from the parent plant.

Seeds need not be swallowed to be spread. Mistletoe seeds stick to beaks and feathers. The birds later scrape them off on different trees.

Fruits spread by mammals—many of whom do not see colors well—look dull but have a strong smell. Fruit bats eat wild mangoes, which hang far out on branches and have an intense smell. This smell helps the night-flying bats locate their food. The bats suck the fruit and spit out the seed. Other fruits may fall to the ground, where small mammals find them by following their noses.

The European rowan and the similar North American mountain ash produce large bright red fruit, a favorite of many birds, such as this Bohemian waxwing.

Colorful fruits

Fruit colors range from pale, waxy yellow to royal red and dark purple. The same chemicals that color flowers give color to fruits: the pigment families called carotenoids and anthocyanins. Most fruit colors stand out against a background of green leaves.

Firethorn, or *Pyracantha*

Spindle tree

Beautyberry

Crowberry

Seeds carried by birds

Popping seed pods and seeds that fly may travel from a few yards to more than a mile from the parent plant. But seeds transported in the digestive system of a bird can venture many miles—even hundreds of miles in a migrating bird. The seeds survive in the bird's system because of their smooth, tough coats. Eventually the bird releases the seeds in droppings or by throwing them up. The droppings may even act as fertilizer, helping the sprout to grow.

Birds and fruiting plants have evolved together. Some birds have especially large beaks for swallowing small fruits whole. Plants, for their part, have evolved fruits with large seeds and little flesh, encouraging birds to swallow the fruits rather than just peck at them. Some seeds cannot sprout until the bird's digestive system works on the seed coat.

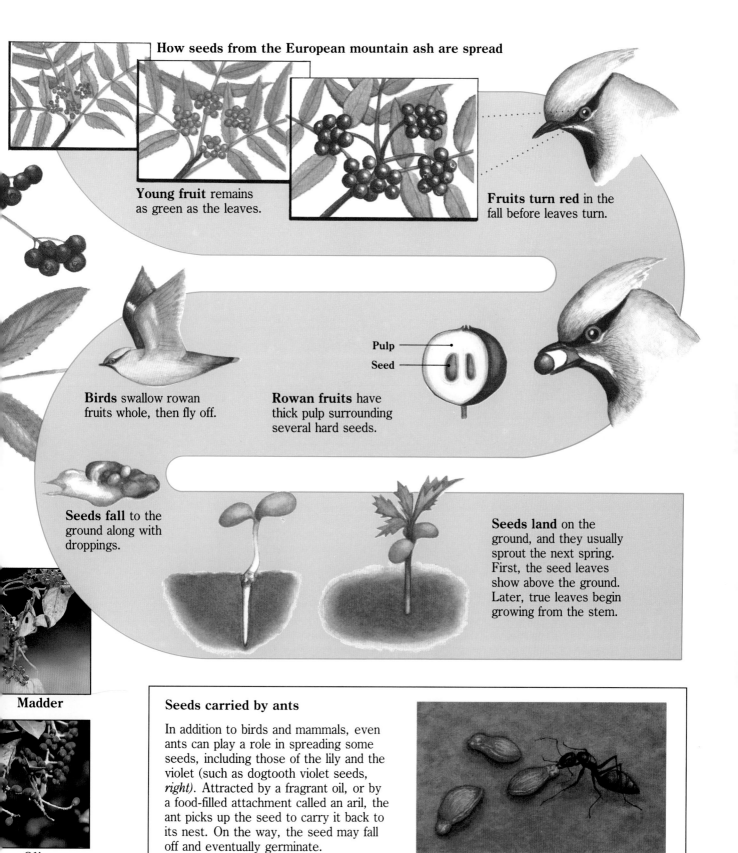

How seeds from the European mountain ash are spread

Young fruit remains as green as the leaves.

Fruits turn red in the fall before leaves turn.

Pulp

Seed

Birds swallow rowan fruits whole, then fly off.

Rowan fruits have thick pulp surrounding several hard seeds.

Seeds fall to the ground along with droppings.

Seeds land on the ground, and they usually sprout the next spring. First, the seed leaves show above the ground. Later, true leaves begin growing from the stem.

Madder

Olive

Seeds carried by ants

In addition to birds and mammals, even ants can play a role in spreading some seeds, including those of the lily and the violet (such as dogtooth violet seeds, *right*). Attracted by a fragrant oil, or by a food-filled attachment called an aril, the ant picks up the seed to carry it back to its nest. On the way, the seed may fall off and eventually germinate.

Can Seeds Sprout on the Tree?

Some seeds do not need to fall to the ground to sprout—they germinate inside the fruit, right on the tree. For instance, mangrove trees, which grow in shallow water along tropical shorelines, would have a problem if they just dropped fruit. The fruit would fall into the sea and float away on the tide—or sink.

Instead, mangrove seeds develop inside the fruit. They grow long roots and may even develop leaves before they drop off the tree. When the seeds finally fall, the roots may be long enough to reach the muddy bottom. Some sprouts will stick in the mud and take root where they fall. Others will float some distance away until their roots drag on the bottom.

The mangrove genus *Kandelia* of Southeast Asia *(left)* grows a single thick root up to a foot in length. When it has grown large enough, the sprout falls off the fruit, stabbing into the mud like a heavy spear.

The mangrove family

Members of the mangrove family (and a few related families) thrive on every continent with tropical shores. Growing up to 100 feet tall, they stand above the water on stiltlike roots. The roots grow through the shallow water into the mud or sand below. Because the tangle of roots catches sand and floating debris, mangroves help to extend the land farther into the ocean.

Petal

Ovary

Root

Mangroves carpet a saltwater beach.

Growth of a *Kandelia* seedling

Kandelia grows right at the water's edge. It blooms in spring, producing flower heads with up to 10 flowers. After pollination, the fruit ripens and the single seed sprouts inside. Growing for nearly a year, the seedling produces a sharp, foot-long root. After falling and sticking in the mud, the tiny seedling sprouts leaves.

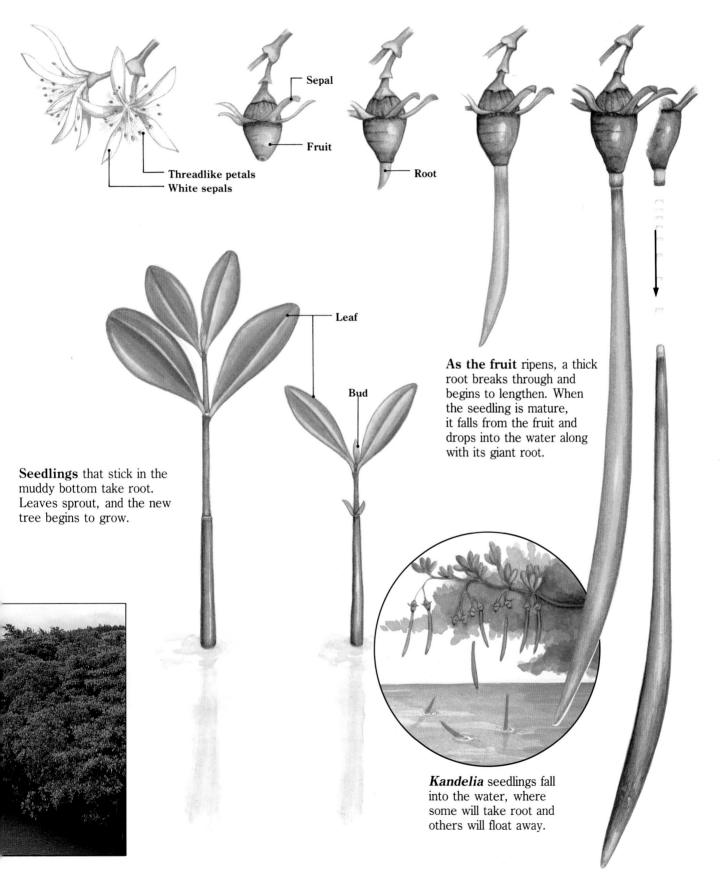

Threadlike petals
White sepals

Sepal
Fruit
Root

Leaf
Bud

Seedlings that stick in the muddy bottom take root. Leaves sprout, and the new tree begins to grow.

As the fruit ripens, a thick root breaks through and begins to lengthen. When the seedling is mature, it falls from the fruit and drops into the water along with its giant root.

Kandelia seedlings fall into the water, where some will take root and others will float away.

How Do Mistletoe Seeds Spread?

Birds spread mistletoe seeds the way they spread seeds of other fruiting plants. But mistletoe has a special need: Only seeds left on tree trunks or branches can sprout. Because mistletoe sends its specialized roots into the tissue of the host tree to get water and minerals, its seeds cannot sprout on the ground.

Occasionally a bird leaves its droppings—along with a few mistletoe seeds—in a tree. But birds also stick seeds onto trees in another way. The mistletoe fruit contains a very sticky sap. When birds eat the fruit, seeds stick to their beaks. Later, when they wipe off the sticky mess against a tree branch, they deposit the seed right where it can sprout best.

Host tree

Mistletoe

Mistletoe is an evergreen parasite that lives on most broad-leaved trees. Although it grows slowly, a single plant may completely surround a branch and grow as big as a barrel.

Mistletoe shows up best in the fall.

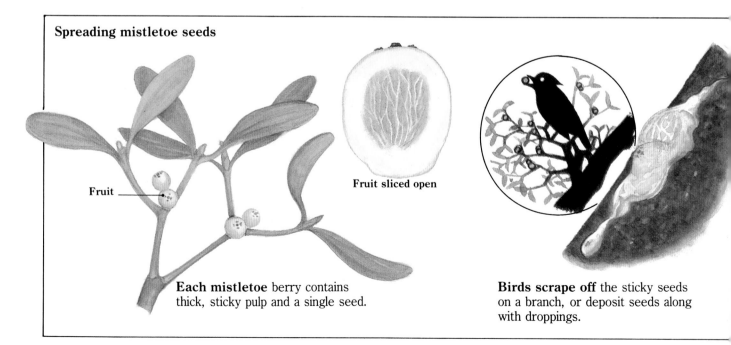

Spreading mistletoe seeds

Fruit

Each mistletoe berry contains thick, sticky pulp and a single seed.

Fruit sliced open

Birds scrape off the sticky seeds on a branch, or deposit seeds along with droppings.

82

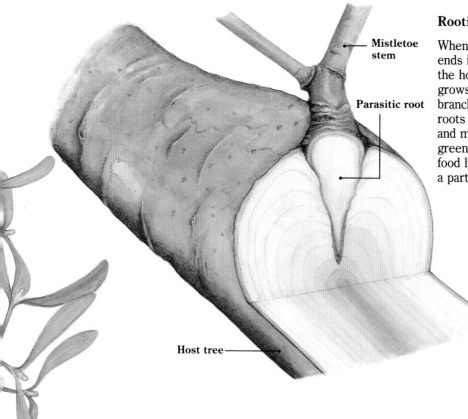

Mistletoe stem

Parasitic root

Host tree

Rooting in a tree

When a mistletoe seed sprouts, the first root ends in a sucker that attaches to the bark of the host tree. A small rootlike protuberance grows from the sucker, slowly entering the branch of the host. Eventually many other roots penetrate the host, sucking up water and minerals. Because mistletoe contains the green pigment chlorophyll and makes its own food like other green plants, botanists call it a partial parasite.

Mistletoe flowers

Mistletoe makes small separate male and female flowers. Both sexes lack petals, although they do have petal-like yellowish sepals. In female flowers, the stigma grows directly up from the ovary. The pollen-bearing anthers grow directly on the insides of the sepals.

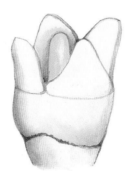

Female flower

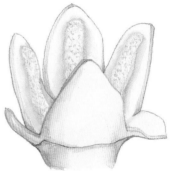

Male flower

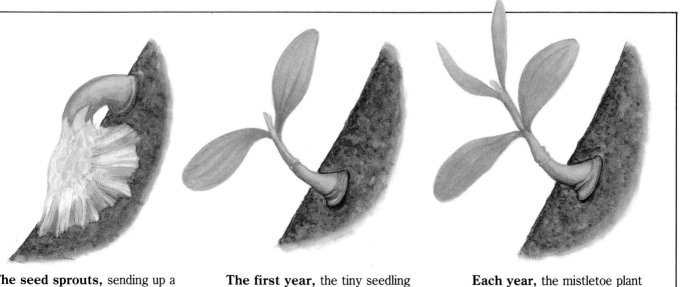

The seed sprouts, sending up a single root to stick to the host's bark with a sucker.

The first year, the tiny seedling makes only one pair of leaves.

Each year, the mistletoe plant grows one new branch point and new leaves.

Why Is Corn Wrapped in Silk?

The silky, threadlike tassels at the tip of an ear of corn are the stigmas and styles. Each kernel of corn—the ovary of a female flower—grows a foot-long style with a long sticky stigma at the tip to catch pollen.

Corn plants grow male flowers at the top of the tall stalk. When the female flowers mature, their stigmas catch pollen blown in the wind. A pollen grain that lands on a stigma must send a pollen tube all the way down the thread to an individual ovary on the cob. After fertilization, the silk turns brownish. The cornhusk, made up of a group of tough, leaflike bracts, protects the fruit.

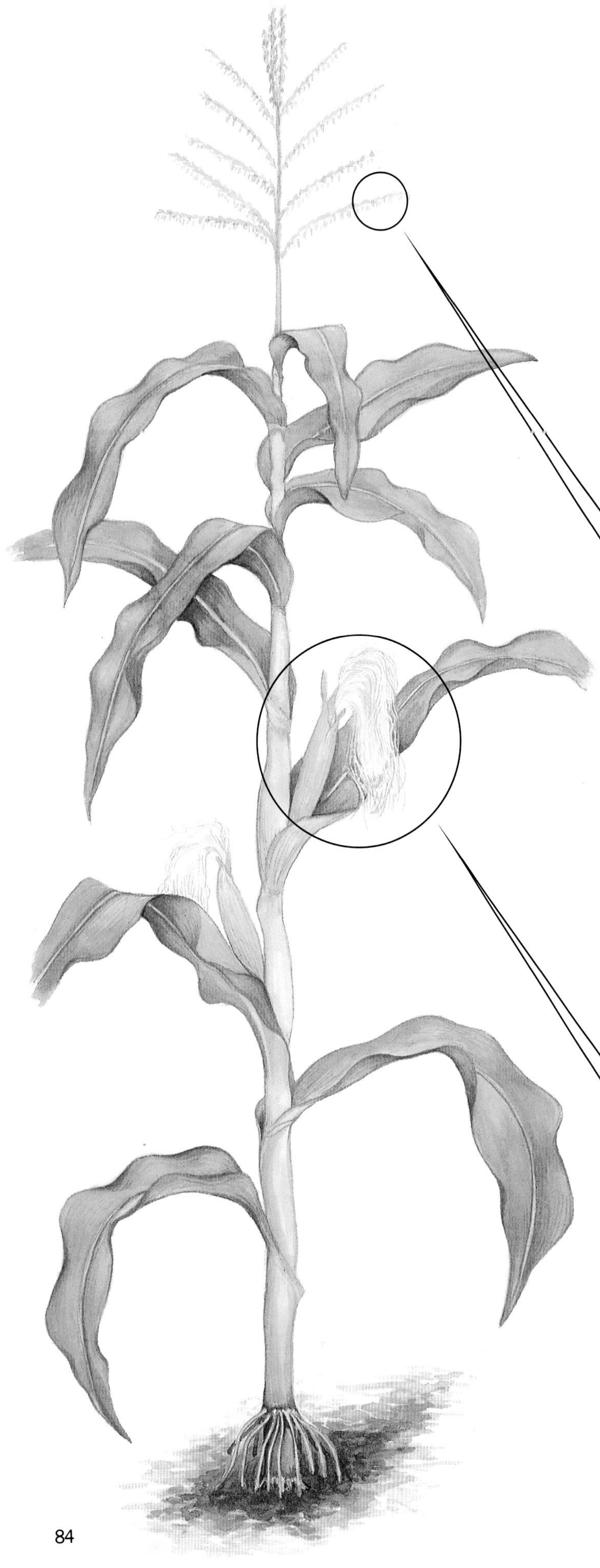

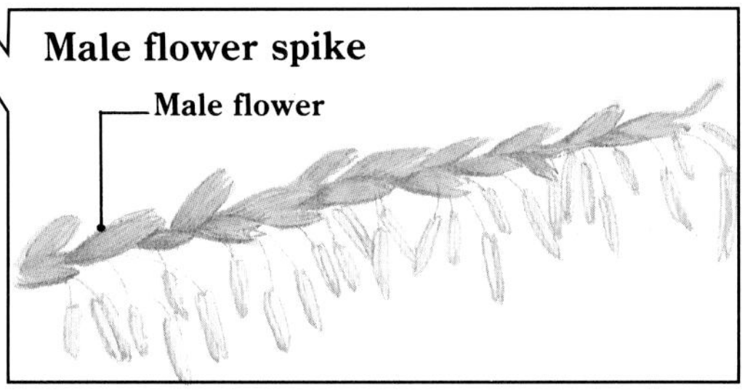

Male flower spike

Male flower

Spikes of male flowers branch out from the tip of the cornstalk. Every male flower has three stamens, each with a large anther.

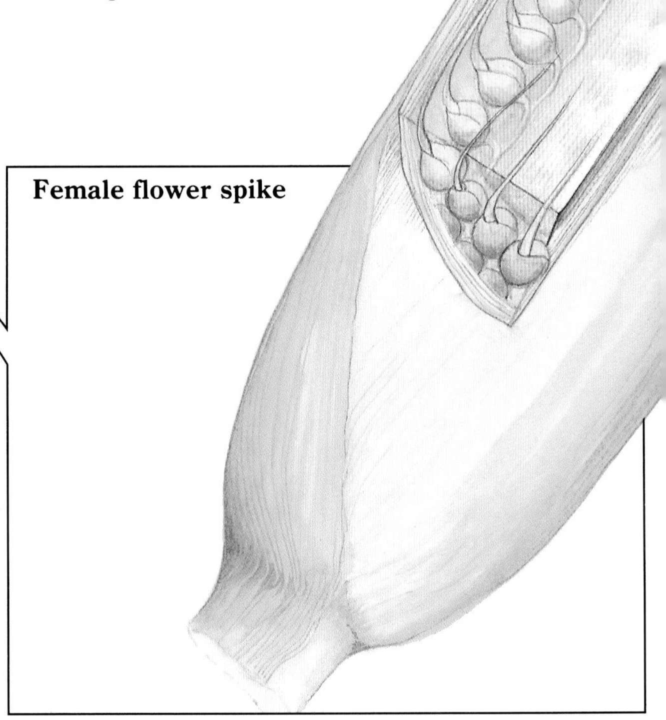

Female flower spike

A spike containing many female flowers grows at the base of each leaf. The flowers form around a stem called the cob.

Inside an ear of corn

Style

Bract

Ovary

Style

The female flower

An individual female corn flower has a single ovary wrapped by a pair of leaflike bracts. From the ovary grows a long style tipped with a sticky stigma to catch pollen.

Ovary

Small bract

Stigma

How corn is pollinated

Corn plants have separate male and female flowers on each plant. The male flowers mature a few days before the female flowers so they won't pollinate female flowers on the same plant. Once the male flowers have shed their pollen and wilted, the female flowers mature. Then the fruit, or corn kernel, develops.

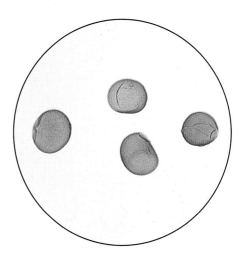

Corn relies on wind to carry pollen from male flowers to the female flowers of a different plant. The tiny, round pollen grains weigh very little. They also have smooth coats to help them sail through the air.

Each ripe corn kernel is a complete fruit, a grain like those of wheat or rice.

What Is a Coconut?

The palm tree, *Cocos nucifera,* produces fruits called coconuts, each with a single seed. The coconut we see in the supermarket consists of a hard shell, which is the inner part of the pericarp, with a seed inside. The white meat inside the seed consists of endosperm, which helps feed the seedling after it sprouts. Coconut milk, a sweet sap, fills a cavity in the endosperm.

When they first fall, coconut fruits look like green footballs, complete with thick, tough coats. The trees grow near the shores in the tropics, and waves may wash the foot-long fruits into the water. They can float for as long as four months before washing up onshore and sprouting.

Structure of a coconut fruit

The coconut fruit is a dry, fibrous kind of drupe. A three-layered pericarp covers the seed. The inner layer is the hard shell. Then comes a fibrous middle layer and a skin that protects the fruit from salt water.

The coconut palm may have originated in Southeast Asia or on the Pacific coast of South America. Coconuts float so far that botanists have had a hard time tracing the origins of this tree. Up to thirty-six 20-foot leaves crown the 100-foot-tall trunk, and separate male and female flowers nestle among the leaves. A single tree may bear coconuts for as long as 80 years.

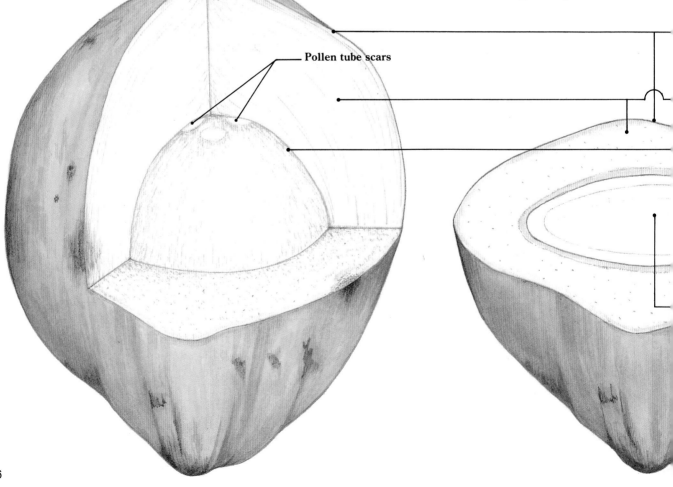

Pollen tube scars

The seafaring coconut fruit

Unique among plants, coconut fruits spread by riding the ocean waves. Though they weigh several pounds, the coconuts still float. Between the waterproof skin and the inner shell lies a thick layer of fibers that traps air. Because the seed may delay sprouting for up to two years, and because the fruit does not absorb water, coconut fruits may drift great distances to finally sprout on a foreign beach.

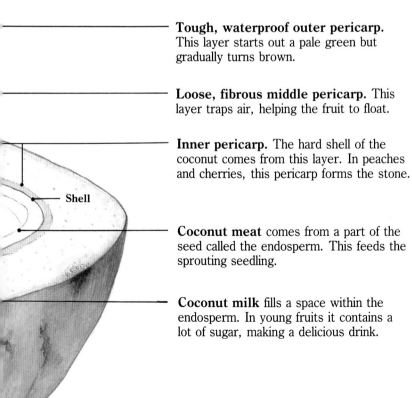

— Shell

Tough, waterproof outer pericarp. This layer starts out a pale green but gradually turns brown.

Loose, fibrous middle pericarp. This layer traps air, helping the fruit to float.

Inner pericarp. The hard shell of the coconut comes from this layer. In peaches and cherries, this pericarp forms the stone.

Coconut meat comes from a part of the seed called the endosperm. This feeds the sprouting seedling.

Coconut milk fills a space within the endosperm. In young fruits it contains a lot of sugar, making a delicious drink.

These coconuts are about to fall.

Are Pine Cones Fruits?

Pine cones do contain seeds, but the hard, scaly cone does not grow from an ovary, so botanists do not call it a fruit. The seeds of evergreen trees—such as pines, firs, cedars, spruces, and redwoods—have no ovary tissue surrounding them, and therefore no fruits.

The scientific names for conifers and their relatives, as well as for flowering plants, describe their seeds. Conifers belong to the group called gymnosperms, from the Greek for "naked" and "seed." Flowering plants are all angiosperms, from the Greek for "container" and "seed." The container, or carpel, develops into the fruit.

Female pine cones actually consist of woody, leaflike bracts, or scales, that protect the seeds. Some gymnosperms make cones so small that they look like berries or small fruits.

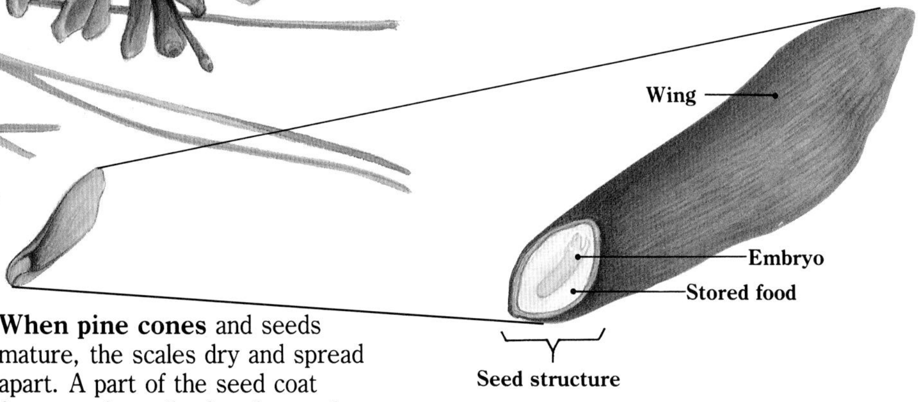

Wing

Embryo

Stored food

Seed structure

When pine cones and seeds mature, the scales dry and spread apart. A part of the seed coat forms a wing, allowing the seed to spiral away on the wind.

A seed that lands on the proper soil will sprout. A root grows first, followed by the seed leaves and finally by true needles.

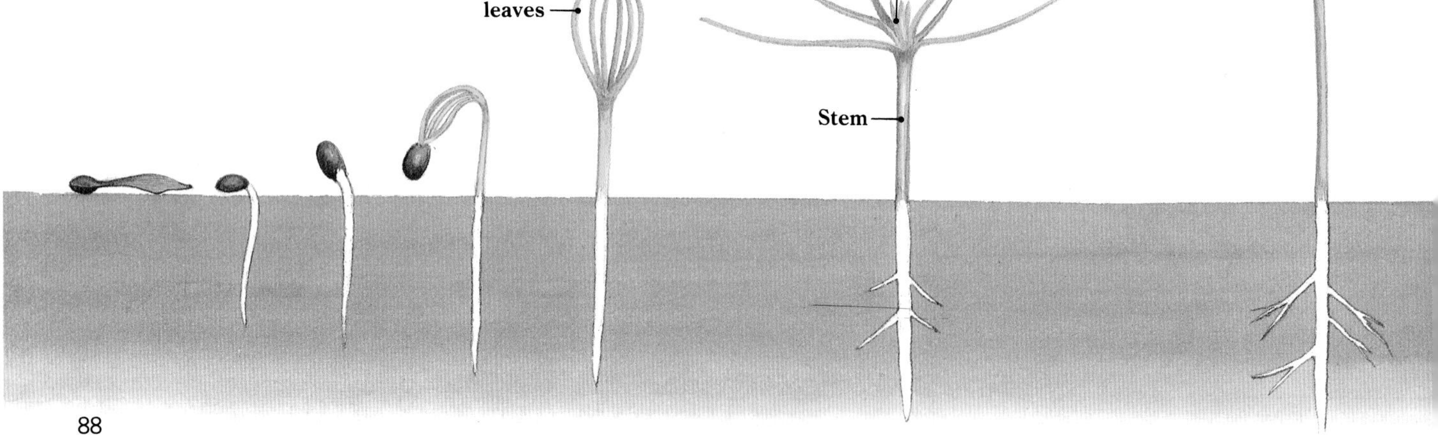

Seed leaves

True needles

Stem

Pollination in pines

Separate female and male flowers, or cones, grow on each pine tree. Female flowers—each scale is like a single flower on a spike—grow at the tips of new branches, and male flower spikes grow at the base of each branch. A male cone produces up to 10 million pollen grains, blown on the wind. When pollen falls on a female cone, it pollinates eggs at the base of each scale. But a year may pass before the pollen fertilizes the eggs and they begin to develop into winged seeds.

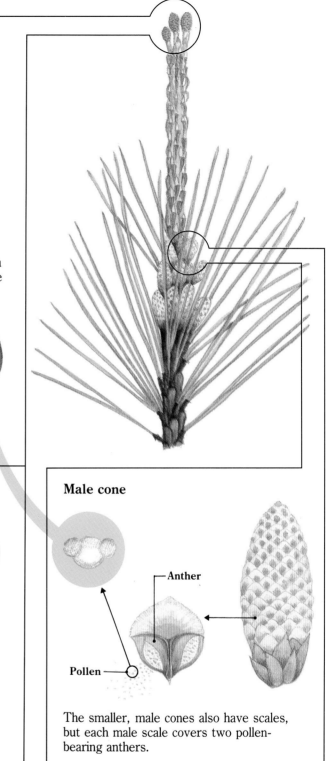

Japanese black pine cone

The hard scales overlap like tiles on a roof, protecting the seeds. Each scale covers two seeds.

Scale

Undeveloped seed

Pollination

Female cone

Scale

Mature seed

Fertilization ends about a year after pollination. Then the scales grow and harden, and the pair of seeds under each scale matures.

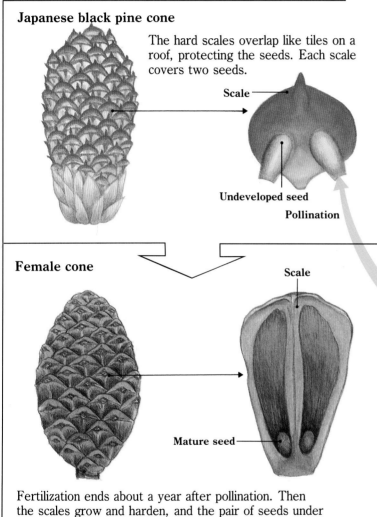

Male cone

Anther

Pollen

The smaller, male cones also have scales, but each male scale covers two pollen-bearing anthers.

Cones of different species

Himalayan cedar cone

Banks' pine cone

Japanese larch cone

***Cryptomeria* cone**

Japanese cypress cone

Can Plants Reproduce without Seeds?

Many plants can reproduce without making flowers and seeds. In some cases, a tiny new plant just grows from some part of the parent plant. Some species sprout new members from leaves, others from stems that grow along the ground. Still others make special underground stems or bulbs that can grow into new plants.

A plant can reproduce without seeds because some of the plant's cells remain unspecialized. Under the right circumstances, these "plain" cells can begin to divide. Their daughter cells can then develop into all of the specialized cells needed to form a complete plant.

No matter how plants reproduce without seeds, all the offspring will have exactly the same genes as the parent. This process, called vegetative reproduction, saves the energy used to make flowers and seeds and gives the sprout nutrition from the parent. But it has some disadvantages. Vegetative sprouts cannot spread very far from the parent plant. And, because they are all identical, they may not survive changes in the environment.

New plant bud

Buds become new plants

Some species in the stonecrop family grow tiny plants on the edges of their scalloped leaves. After the sprouts have grown tiny leaves and roots, they fall to the ground, sometimes traveling a little in the wind. Each new plant will be genetically identical to the parent.

Stonecrop, or *Sedum,* originally came from Asia. Now it thrives throughout the United States and Europe and is a popular plant for rock gardens.

Spreading on the surface

Many plants grow thin stems, called runners, that flop down along the ground. Where the stem touches the ground, it may take root and sprout leaves.

Runners

Strawberries spread by sending runners along the ground, forming new plants.

Bud

Tiny bulb

This lily variety grows tiny buds at the tips of its leaves. Each bud can grow into a complete plant.

Yams grow small buds along their stems. Each bud can sprout roots and leaves, developing into a complete plant.

Another lily variety grows tiny bulbs at the bases of its leaves. Each minibulb can become a complete plant.

Spreading underground

Some plants spread underground. Onionlike bulbs store food and grow tiny new bulbs on their surfaces. Underground stems, called rhizomes and tubers, and swollen stalks growing just underground, called corms, can all produce new plants.

Potato plants store food in swollen underground stems called tubers. Tiny plants, or eyes, sprout from the surface of the tuber.

Shoot growing from eye

Roots

Corm

Bulb

Potato tuber

Bamboo and other grasses spread rapidly with underground stems known as rhizomes.

Rhizome

Bamboo shoot

Tulips grow from bulbs, a sort of underground bud. Fleshy leaves surround the bud. Bulbs often split or bud off smaller bulbs.

Gladiolus plants grow from thickened underground stems called corms. New corms may bud off the surface.

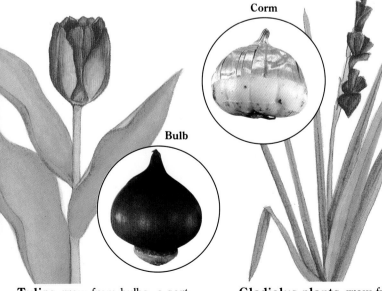

6
Plants without Flowers

The nonflowering plants, a small but important group within the plant kingdom, are not as complex as their flowering counterparts. They usually lack the specialized roots, stems, and leaves of higher plants. Many of them also lack chlorophyll and do not go through photosynthesis. Without a way to manufacture food, they must live off other plants and animals as parasites, absorbing nutrients from the bodies of their hosts.

What sets these plants even further apart is the way they propagate. Their reproduction does not involve seeds but begins with spores instead,

in a process known as alternation of generations *(pages 94-95)*.

Nonflowering plants have played an important role in the evolution of life. About 3.5 billion years ago, with the emergence of the simplest life forms on Earth, the atmosphere consisted mainly of carbon dioxide. The atmosphere changed some 500,000 years later when the slightly more evolved blue-green algae appeared. The algae absorbed carbon dioxide during photosynthesis and released oxygen as a by-product. As plants developed and adapted to growth on land, they evolved other nonflowering species, such as ferns, mosses, and horsetails. The atmosphere filled with increasing amounts of oxygen, setting the stage for the appearance of oxygen-breathing animals.

Some easily recognized nonflowering plants include mosses *(upper left)*, liverworts *(upper right)*, and mushrooms and toadstools *(below)*.

How Are Spores Different from Seeds?

In flowering plants, pollen combines with an ovule within the flower to produce a seed. When the seed germinates, it grows into a plant identical to the one that created it. But the nonflowering plants, which include mosses, ferns, fungi, and algae, reproduce in different ways.

These plants begin life as sporophytes, plants that produce asexual spores, which are similar to seeds but contain only half the genetic information of a seed. When these spores germinate, they produce a new plant generation called gametophyte. The gametophytes produce the gametes, or reproductive cells, which are either male or female. When a male and a female gamete join in a body of water, they produce a fertilized egg, called a zygote. The zygote germinates into a sporophyte, which begins the process—called alternation of generations—all over again.

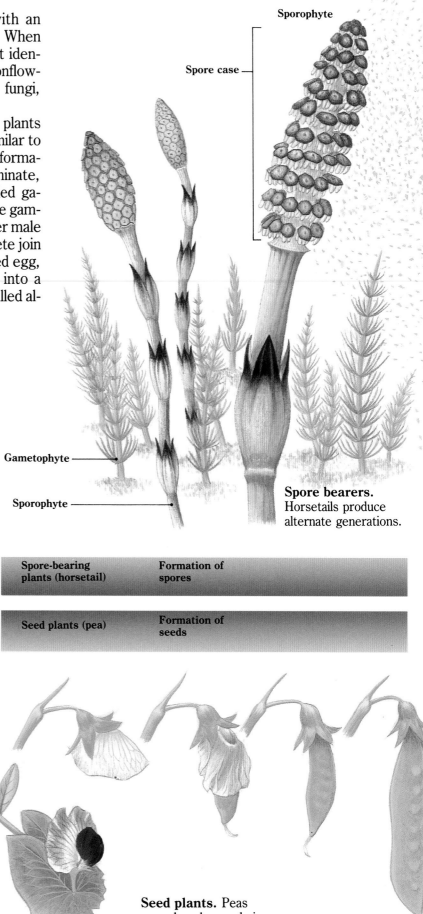

Sporophyte

Spore case

Gametophyte

Sporophyte

Spore bearers. Horsetails produce alternate generations.

Spore-bearing plants (horsetail)	Formation of spores

Seed plants (pea)	Formation of seeds

From spores to seeds

The evolution of plants on Earth began with one-celled microorganisms, which appeared in the seas in the Precambrian era some 3.5 billion years ago. From those simple aquatic plants evolved the first generation of terrestrial plants. These newly land-bound plants reproduced by spores in a process that still required water. In order to spread across dry land, some 400 million years ago they slowly changed the mechanism by which they reproduced, and they evolved as seed plants.

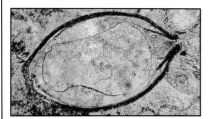

The fossilized cedar tree seed *(above)* dates to the Carboniferous period of the Paleozoic era, some 350 million years ago.

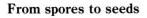

Seed plants. Peas reproduce by seeds in sexual reproduction.

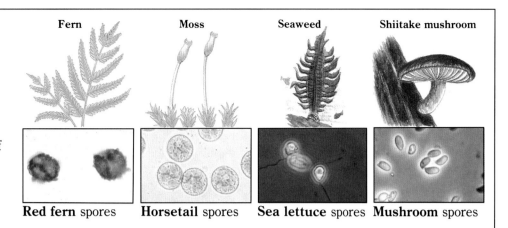

Spore-producing plants

Botanists estimate that there are about 450,000 species of plants on Earth. Of those, some 125,000 reproduce by seeds, while the rest propagate by spores. All spore-bearing plants belong to one of four classes: ferns, mosses, algae, or fungi.

Fern

Moss

Seaweed

Shiitake mushroom

Red fern spores **Horsetail** spores **Sea lettuce** spores **Mushroom** spores

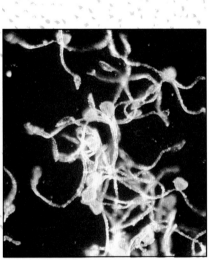

Spores divide to form four cells with one representative of each chromosome.

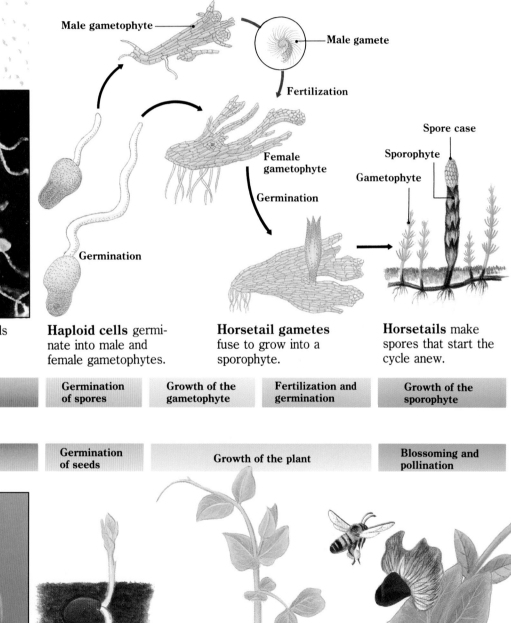

Male gametophyte

Male gamete

Fertilization

Germination

Female gametophyte

Germination

Gametophyte

Sporophyte

Spore case

Haploid cells germinate into male and female gametophytes.

Horsetail gametes fuse to grow into a sporophyte.

Horsetails make spores that start the cycle anew.

| Spore | Germination of spores | Growth of the gametophyte | Fertilization and germination | Growth of the sporophyte |

| Seed | Germination of seeds | Growth of the plant | Blossoming and pollination |

Seeds are self-contained, possessing all necessary genetic and nutritive material for germination.

When a seed germinates, it grows into a plant like the one that produced it.

Flowers emerge and bloom; then pollen fertilizes the egg, causing new seeds to develop.

How Can Fungi Get Food?

Fungi are a class of spore-producing plants that cannot produce food through photosynthesis, as green plants do. Rather, they live as parasites, growing on plants and animals and absorbing nutrients from them. Some also thrive on decaying plant and animal remains; these organisms are known as saprophytes. A common type of saprophytic fungus is the mushroom, which can be found on dead trees and fallen leaves.

Botanists speculate that there are some 70,000 species of fungi, falling into two classes: Eumycetes and Myxomycetes. Eumycetes encompass the true fungi: the mushrooms, truffles, rusts, powdery mildews, and bread molds. Their immobile bodies consist of branched filaments called hyphae. The Myxomycetes fungi, or slime molds, spend part of their lives as amoeba-like organisms called plasmodia. These creatures slide over decaying matter in search of bacteria and organic particles to feed on. Because they can feed themselves, Myxomycetes fungi are sometimes said to be animals rather than plants, but they also have a stationary plantlike stage in which they produce spores.

Feeding on foods

Mold is the collective term given to fungi that are not mushrooms. These organisms grow on and get their nutrition from such foods as fruits, vegetables, and grains. By secreting an enzyme, they break the food down into simple organic molecules that they can readily absorb. As they eat, the molds grow larger by extending branched filaments.

Different types of mold secrete various enzymes, each of which works best on a specific food. Fruits and vegetables, for example, are good hosts for cobweb molds and fur molds, while carbohydrate-rich foods such as bread are favored by the aspergillus mold.

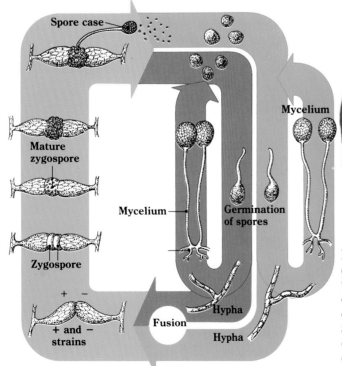

Fungi such as the cobweb mold (*right*) are spore-bearing plants that alternate generations. Spores disseminate to produce mycelia of different sexual strains, denoted as + or −, which fuse to develop a zygospore that then produces a spore body.

Cobweb mold

Fungi that feast on bacteria

Slime molds are a special type of fungi. They begin as slimy, jellylike cells called plasmodia that slowly crawl along decaying matter, such as rotting trees and leaves, and ingest any bacteria, protozoa, and organic substances they encounter. Once they grow to maturity, they become immobile and grow spore cases, which produce and release male and female spores. When the spores germinate, they produce amoeba-like cells called swarm cells. These fuse in pairs to form a zygote, or fertilized egg, that develops into a plasmodium. All fungi that exist as plasmodia are referred to as myxomycetes.

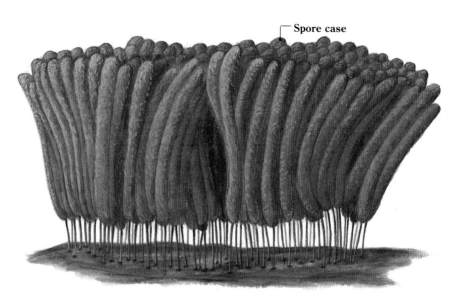

Spore case

A plasmodium cell contains a full complement of genetic material, an amount denoted by scientists as *2n*. When the cell matures and releases spores, each spore has only half the genetic material, represented by an *n*.

Spore case

Plasmodium

Young plasmodium

2n myxamoeba or swarm cell

n myxamoeba or swarm cell

Fusion

n

Spore produces swarm cell

Swarm cell

Spore fruit

Stalk of spore fruit

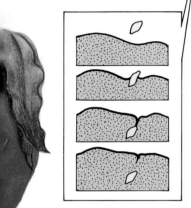

A plasmodium encountering a bacterium surrounds and engulfs it. Once inside, the bacterium is digested by special enzymes.

Fungi that live off insects

A number of fungus species have evolved so that they can live off insects. The cicada fungus, for example, lives on cicada larvae. When a larva dies, the fungus obtains nutrition from its body and sends growths above ground. These growths, called spore fruits, contain structures called perithecia, which are divided into chambers called asci. Within each ascus reside eight spores.

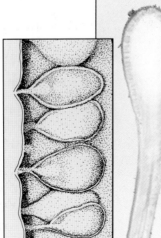

Great numbers of perithecia can be found on each spore fruit.

Dead cicada larva

How Do Mushrooms Grow?

A mushroom is the fruiting body, or sporophore, that grows from certain types of fungi. The structure arises from a bulbous growth at the base, called a volva, and extends in a stalklike trunk, or stem, to end in an umbrella-like pileus, or cap. The point at which the top of the cap breaks free is called the annulus, or ring. Underneath the cap, radiating outward from the center, are a series of ridges known as gills, on which spores form. When the spores fall from the gills, they disperse in the wind and eventually take root to form new fungi and mushrooms.

The death cap is a beautiful but *poisonous* mushroom that grows in open woods. Poisonous mushrooms such as the death cap are commonly called toadstools.

Cap

Ring

Stem

A wide world of mushrooms

There are many different classes of fungi, but from only two of these classes do mushrooms and related plants grow: Basidiomycetes and Ascomycetes. Mushrooms and toadstools, with their distinctive stems and umbrella-like caps, grow from Basidiomycetes fungi. Somewhat similar looking and closely related to the mushrooms are truffles, which grow from Ascomycetes fungi. Shown at near right is a cup fungus, one of the Ascomycetes fungi, and the Jew's ear and earthstar mushrooms, both puffballs grown from Basidiomycetes fungi.

Cup fungus

Jew's ear

Life cycle of a mushroom

A mushroom produces spores in structures called basidia, located on the gills underneath the mushroom's cap. Each spore can be one of two sexes, shown as + or −. When a spore of either sex falls from a mushroom and lands on rotting matter—such as a fallen tree or decaying leaves—it germinates and grows into a chain of cells called a primary mycelium. When primary mycelia generated by + and − spores meet, they conjugate, or bond together, to form a secondary mycelium.

Feeding on nutrients from the decaying matter, the secondary mycelium forms a small cluster of mycelia known as a volva, which gradually develops into a mushroom. The newly sprouted mushroom forms spores of its own, and the process begins anew.

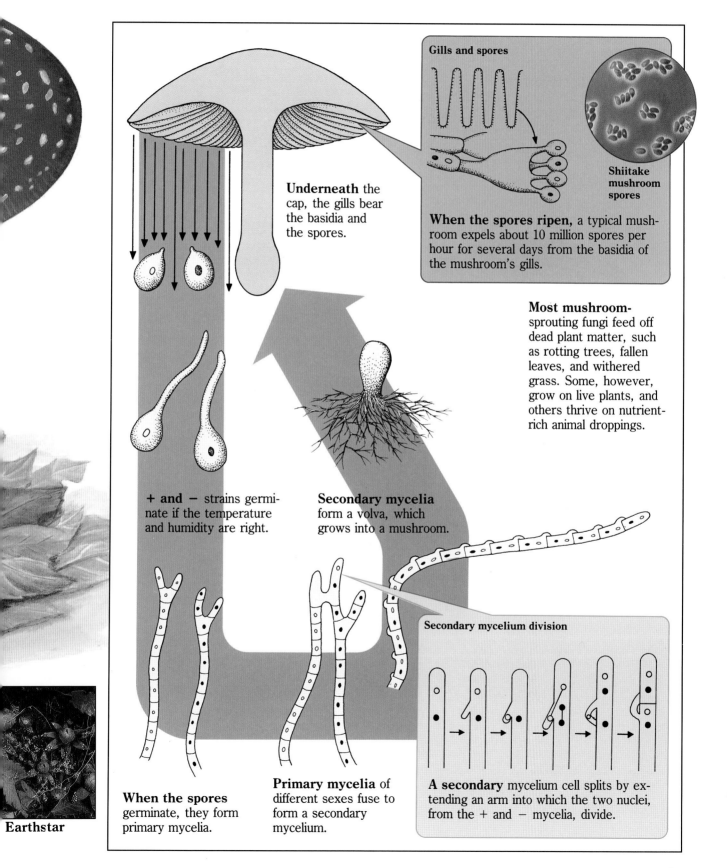

Gills and spores

When the spores ripen, a typical mushroom expels about 10 million spores per hour for several days from the basidia of the mushroom's gills.

Shiitake mushroom spores

Underneath the cap, the gills bear the basidia and the spores.

Most mushroom-sprouting fungi feed off dead plant matter, such as rotting trees, fallen leaves, and withered grass. Some, however, grow on live plants, and others thrive on nutrient-rich animal droppings.

+ and − strains germinate if the temperature and humidity are right.

Secondary mycelia form a volva, which grows into a mushroom.

Secondary mycelium division

When the spores germinate, they form primary mycelia.

Primary mycelia of different sexes fuse to form a secondary mycelium.

A secondary mycelium cell splits by extending an arm into which the two nuclei, from the + and − mycelia, divide.

Earthstar

What Is a Diatom?

Diatoms are tiny one-celled algae that live in water. Like all other green plants, they contain chlorophyll, which they use to convert sunlight into energy through the process of photosynthesis. These plants are an essential part of the world's food chain, for they are consumed by marine life, great and small, up to the largest whales in the world.

To protect its single, soft cell, a diatom secretes a hard substance that forms a surrounding shell. The shell consists of top and bottom halves, with the top fitting like a lid over the bottom. The shells are coated with delicately sculptured glasslike silica. The patterns fall into one of two categories: radial, in which the pattern moves symmetrically outward from the center; and pinnate, in which the pattern forms two mirror images separated by a central axis.

Structure of a diatom

Diatoms lie encased in shells that are unique to each species.

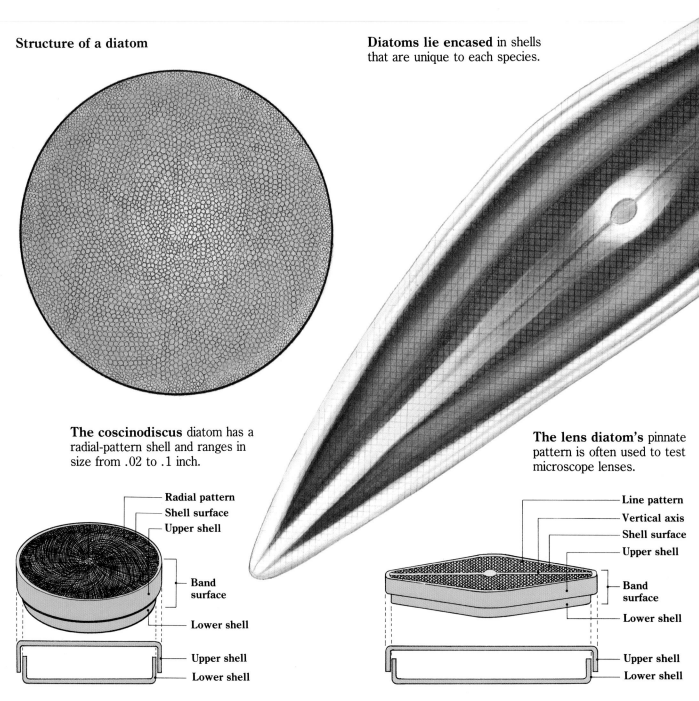

The coscinodiscus diatom has a radial-pattern shell and ranges in size from .02 to .1 inch.

The lens diatom's pinnate pattern is often used to test microscope lenses.

Radial pattern
Shell surface
Upper shell
Band surface
Lower shell
Upper shell
Lower shell

Line pattern
Vertical axis
Shell surface
Upper shell
Band surface
Lower shell
Upper shell
Lower shell

Diatom reproduction

Diatoms have an unusual pattern of reproduction. The process begins as a diatom cell divides in two, and the top and bottom shells split. Each new cell takes one of the shells to use as its top and then grows a new bottom. This results in two new diatoms, one the same size as the original—the one from the top shell of the parent—and one smaller—the one from the bottom shell. Over the course of successive divisions, the shells will eventually become too small to divide in this way. When this happens, two tiny diatoms fuse together to form a new, larger diatom, which can then reproduce in the conventional manner.

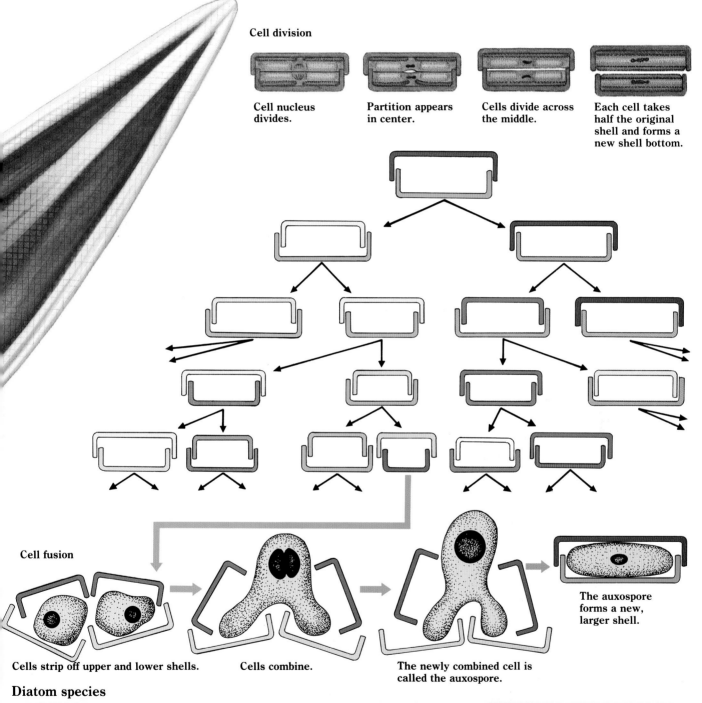

Cell division

Cell nucleus divides.

Partition appears in center.

Cells divide across the middle.

Each cell takes half the original shell and forms a new shell bottom.

Cell fusion

Cells strip off upper and lower shells.

Cells combine.

The newly combined cell is called the auxospore.

The auxospore forms a new, larger shell.

Diatom species

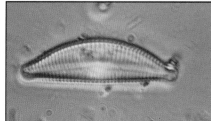

Cymbella

Synedra

Tabellaria

How Do Algae Reproduce?

Algae is the collective name given to aquatic plants that lack specialized body parts, such as roots, stems, and leaves. Algae range in size from microscopic diatoms *(pages 100-101)* to 100-foot-long blades of kelp. They grow in virtually all the world's seas, making their home in both salt and fresh water from tropical to polar latitudes. All algae contain chlorophyll and produce food through photosynthesis.

Algae reproduce by several means. Whereas unicellular algae go through simple cell division, multicellular species propagate by spores and gametes through alternation of generations *(pages 94-95),* in which the two different generations are identical. This is the simplest form of sexual reproduction and is known as isomorphism. But in a few species, most notably kelp, there is a dramatic difference between the sporophyte and gametophyte generations—a phenomenon known as heteromorphism.

Reproduction of algae

Sea lettuce

In a subtle alternation, the *Ulva pertussa* algae produce sporophyte and gametophyte generations that look alike.

Male and female gametes from the gametophyte join to produce a zygote.

A zygote will germinate and grow into a sporophyte as soon as it adheres to a rock or other stable foundation.

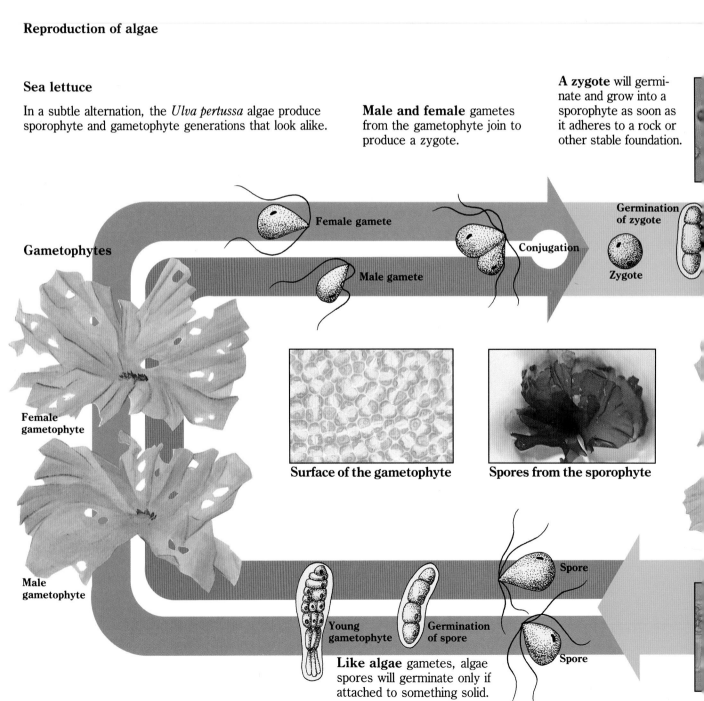

Gametophytes

Female gamete

Male gamete

Conjugation

Germination of zygote

Zygote

Female gametophyte

Male gametophyte

Surface of the gametophyte

Spores from the sporophyte

Spore

Young gametophyte

Germination of spore

Spore

Like algae gametes, algae spores will germinate only if attached to something solid.

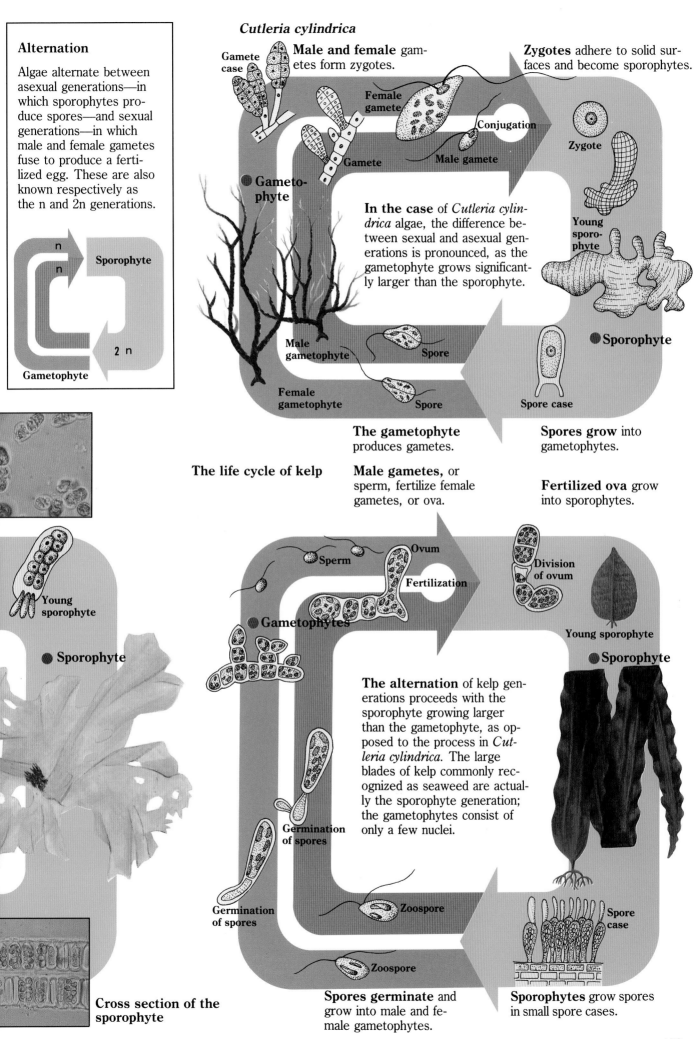

Alternation

Algae alternate between asexual generations—in which sporophytes produce spores—and sexual generations—in which male and female gametes fuse to produce a fertilized egg. These are also known respectively as the n and 2n generations.

n
n
Sporophyte
2 n
Gametophyte

Cutleria cylindrica

Male and female gametes form zygotes.

Gamete case

Female gamete

Conjugation

Gamete

Male gamete

Gameto-phyte

Zygotes adhere to solid surfaces and become sporophytes.

Zygote

Young sporophyte

In the case of *Cutleria cylindrica* algae, the difference between sexual and asexual generations is pronounced, as the gametophyte grows significantly larger than the sporophyte.

Sporophyte

Male gametophyte

Spore

Female gametophyte

Spore

Spore case

The gametophyte produces gametes.

Spores grow into gametophytes.

The life cycle of kelp

Male gametes, or sperm, fertilize female gametes, or ova.

Fertilized ova grow into sporophytes.

Young sporophyte

Sporophyte

Cross section of the sporophyte

Sperm

Ovum

Fertilization

Gametophytes

Division of ovum

Young sporophyte

Sporophyte

Germination of spores

Germination of spores

The alternation of kelp generations proceeds with the sporophyte growing larger than the gametophyte, as opposed to the process in *Cutleria cylindrica.* The large blades of kelp commonly recognized as seaweed are actually the sporophyte generation; the gametophytes consist of only a few nuclei.

Zoospore

Zoospore

Spore case

Spores germinate and grow into male and female gametophytes.

Sporophytes grow spores in small spore cases.

Do Seaweeds Undergo Photosynthesis?

Seaweed is the name for algae that live in seawater. Like most land plants, seaweeds create energy through photosynthesis. The raw materials for this process are readily available: Water is absorbed directly into the seaweed, along with the carbon dioxide that is dissolved in the water. The sun's rays that penetrate the water's surface provide enough light to catalyze the reaction.

Seaweed's watery environment adds an unusual wrinkle to photosynthesis. When sunlight passes through air, all seven of its component colors—red, orange, yellow, green, blue, indigo, and violet—travel in unison. But in water, some components pass through more easily than others. For this reason, many seaweeds have evolved "auxiliary pigments" *(opposite)* that aid in the absorption of specific components of sunlight, making photosynthesis more efficient.

Seaweed photosynthesis

Solar rays

Solar rays

Solar rays

Solar rays

Water

Carbon dioxide

Water

Carbon dioxide

Water

Anatomy of a seaweed

Seaweeds are simple plants. They lack the highly differentiated roots, stems, and leaves of their land-rooted counterparts, as well as the complex system of vascular bundles through which nutrients flow. While conventional plants absorb nutrients through their roots, seaweeds absorb them through their entire bodies.

Trophophylls are the tendrils that extend from a blade of seaweed.

Sporophylls contain the seaweed's reproductive organs.

A seaweed's base anchors the plant to a rock or other solid object on the seafloor.

The *Undarid pinnatifida* seaweed shown at right is a type of brown algae that can grow as long as seven feet.

Photosynthesis under the sea

Plants that live on land undergo photosynthesis to convert water, carbon dioxide, and sunlight into starch. But in seaweed, photosynthesis creates a number of additional nutrients *(below)*.

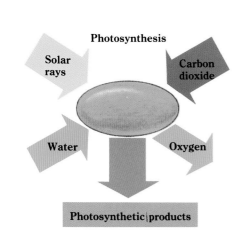

Photosynthesis

Solar rays

Carbon dioxide

Water

Oxygen

Photosynthetic products

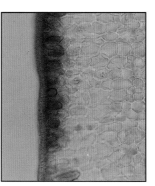

Brown algae cells

The role of pigments

In addition to the chlorophyll that all green plants possess, many algae have auxiliary pigments that aid in the absorption of various colors of light. All algae belong to one of three major classes, according to their pigments.

Green algae contain mostly chlorophyll a and b, pigments that absorb red and orange light well and give the algae a green tint.

Enteromorpha linza

Thick-haired *Codium*

| Chlorophyll a |
| Chlorophyll b |

Photosynthesis

| Starch |

Brown algae, like sea fans, get their color from an auxiliary pigment called fucoxanthin, which is a good absorber of green light.

Brown algae

Sea fan

| Chlorophyll a |
| Chlorophyll b |
| Fucoxanthin |

Photosynthesis

| Mannitol Laminarin |

Red algae owe their color to an auxiliary pigment called phyco-erythrin. This pigment makes red algae excellent absorbers of blue and violet light.

Scinaia latifrons

Pachymeniopsis elliptica

| Chlorophyll a |
| Phycoerythrin |

Photosynthesis

| Floridean starch |

Depth and distribution

Because the sunlight needed for photosynthesis cannot penetrate far through water, most sea-weeds live at shallow depths. About 70 percent live in the so-called intertidal zone, between the high- and low-tide lines.

Different components of sunlight, however, travel farther through water than others. The violet component reaches down the farthest, so algae efficient at absorbing this color of light—such as red algae—can flourish at greater depths in the sublittoral zone. Green algae, which are good absorbers of sunlight's red and orange components, must live closer to the surface, because those wavelengths do not penetrate water well.

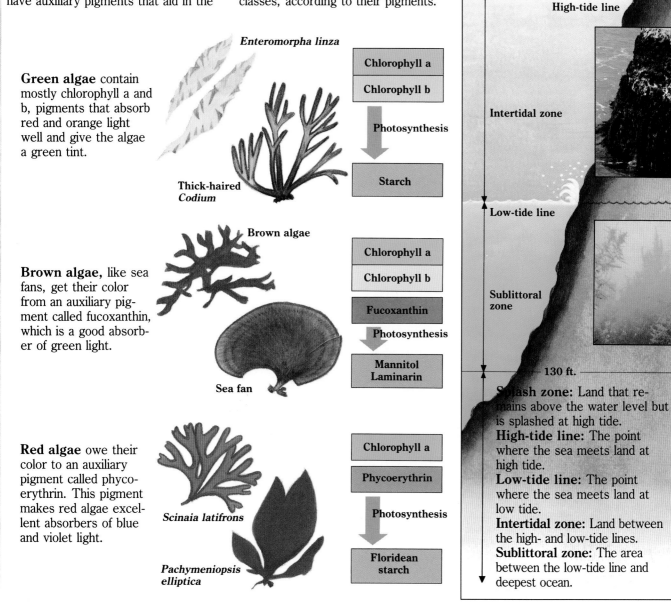

Splash zone

High-tide line

Intertidal zone

Low-tide line

Sublittoral zone

— 130 ft. —

Splash zone: Land that remains above the water level but is splashed at high tide.
High-tide line: The point where the sea meets land at high tide.
Low-tide line: The point where the sea meets land at low tide.
Intertidal zone: Land between the high- and low-tide lines.
Sublittoral zone: The area between the low-tide line and deepest ocean.

What Are Lichens?

Lichens are unusual dual organisms that consist of algae living together with fungi. This arrangement is known as mutualism, a type of symbiosis in which the two species help each other to survive. In the case of lichens, the algae provide fungi with nourishment generated through photosynthesis, while the fungi provide water and essential minerals for the algae. Together, they are stronger than either would be separately; the relationship allows lichens to flourish at extremes of temperature and humidity that would normally spell death for an algae or fungus living alone.

There are approximately 15,000 different types of lichens, composed of varying fungi and algae. Most of the algae are of the blue-green variety *(pages 92-93),* and the vast majority of the fungi are sac fungi of the Ascomycetes class *(pages 98-99).* They can combine to create wildly varied lichens. Some attach themselves solidly to rocks and tree trunks and spread outward, some grow upward, and still others dangle loosely from the limbs of trees.

Lichens have three structural layers: the cortex, a layer of hard fungus cells; the gonidium layer, mainly algae; and the pith, where much of the reproduction takes place. Some lichens also have a lower cortex.

Lichens reproduce in two ways. In asexual reproduction, cell buds, or soredia, extend from the original growth and break loose. For sexual reproduction, a fruiting body called an ascocarp produces spores.

Rhizocarpon lichen adheres to rocks at high altitudes.

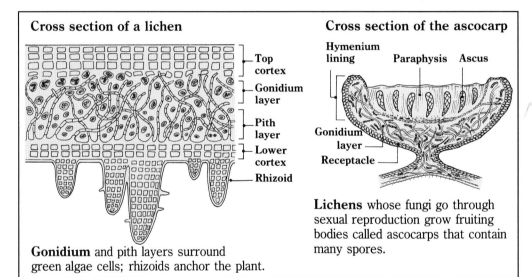

Cross section of a lichen

- Top cortex
- Gonidium layer
- Pith layer
- Lower cortex
- Rhizoid

Gonidium and pith layers surround green algae cells; rhizoids anchor the plant.

Cross section of the ascocarp

Hymenium lining • Paraphysis • Ascus • Gonidium layer • Receptacle

Lichens whose fungi go through sexual reproduction grow fruiting bodies called ascocarps that contain many spores.

Wartlike, or crustaceous, lichens grow on rocks and trees in scablike patterns. They anchor tenaciously to their hosts and are difficult to pry loose. The *Rhizocarpon* below is a typical crustaceous lichen.

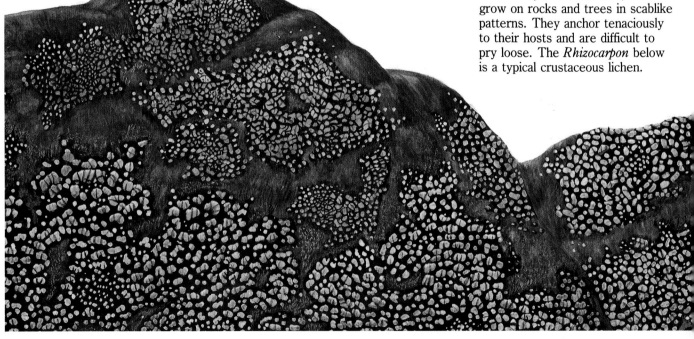

Arborescent lichens

A number of lichens, called arborescent lichens, either grow upright like trees or hang from tree branches.

Cortex
Gonidium layer
Pith layer
Axis

The old-man's-beard lichen *(above)* adheres to the bark of needle-leaf trees in coniferous forests.

The shield lichen *(right)* adheres to pine and plum trees.

Thallus lichens *(right)* adhere to rocks and tree bark. They have flat bodies that look like leaves, with their surface appearing distinctly different from the underside.

Algae cells
Fungi cells

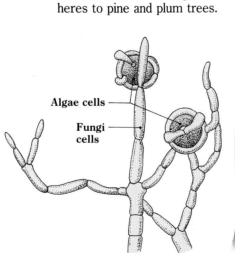

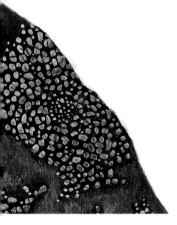

Lichens are the first to grow on lava.

Pioneers of the plant kingdom

When lichens anchor themselves to rocks, they secrete a chemical that turns the rock's surface into a thin, muddy layer on which other types of plants can take root. Because of this chemical, lichens can turn a rocky, barren area—such as a lava field after a volcanic eruption—into an area that is soon teeming with new plant life.

How Do Mosses and Ferns Differ?

Although mosses and ferns are both spore-producing plants that alternate generations, they differ in two major ways. The first concerns the dominant generation. In ferns by far the larger generation—and the more commonly recognized—is the sporophyte, with its long stem and leaflike lobes. The gametophyte, however, is a tiny, one-quarter-inch-long plant that is difficult to spot. The opposite is true with the mosses, and their close relatives, the liverworts, where the gametophyte is dominant.

The other variance lies in the way the generations grow. With ferns, the sporophyte and gametophyte generations are independent of each other. But with mosses and liverworts they are completely dependent: The sporophyte grows out of the gametophyte itself and needs it for its nourishment.

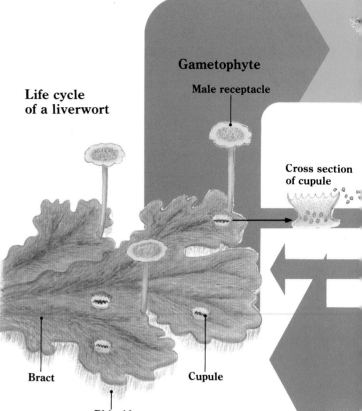

Life cycle of a liverwort

Gametophyte

Male receptacle

Cross section of cupule

Bract

Rhizoid

Cupule

Differences between mosses and ferns

	Mosses	Ferns
Ecology	Hair moss Gametophytes Grow in damp places Produce gametes	Aspidium fern Sporophytes Grow in damp places Produce spores
Morphology	Roots, stems, and leaves are differentiated in some but not in others.	Roots, stems, and leaves are differentiated.
Roots	Rhizoid Rhizoid Rhizoids anchor the plant. They do not function as true roots.	Root Rhizome Root Roots absorb water and nutrients and hold the plant in place.
Stem	Even mosses with stems do not have vascular bundles.	Fern stems have vascular bundles.
Leaves	Mosses absorb water through entire blades.	Ferns absorb water through stomas.

Life cycle of a fern

Common bracken forms dense growths in woods and fields.

Stem

Rhizome

Root

108

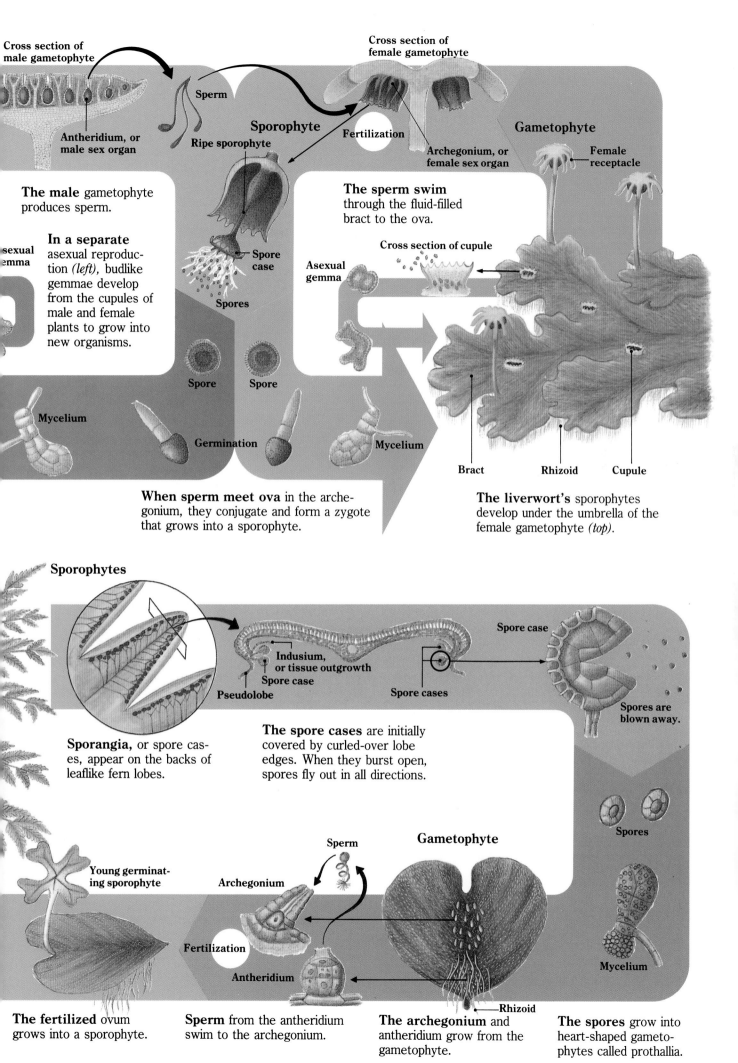

Cross section of
male gametophyte

Sperm

Cross section of
female gametophyte

Antheridium, or
male sex organ

Sporophyte

Ripe sporophyte

Fertilization

Gametophyte

Archegonium, or
female sex organ

Female
receptacle

The male gametophyte
produces sperm.

In a separate
asexual reproduc-
tion *(left),* budlike
gemmae develop
from the cupules of
male and female
plants to grow into
new organisms.

Asexual
gemma

Spore
case

Spores

Spore

Spore

Mycelium

Germination

Mycelium

Asexual
gemma

Cross section of cupule

The sperm swim
through the fluid-filled
bract to the ova.

Bract

Rhizoid

Cupule

When sperm meet ova in the archegonium, they conjugate and form a zygote
that grows into a sporophyte.

The liverwort's sporophytes
develop under the umbrella of the
female gametophyte *(top).*

Sporophytes

Spore case

Indusium,
or tissue outgrowth
Spore case

Pseudolobe

Spore cases

Spores are
blown away.

Sporangia, or spore cases, appear on the backs of
leaflike fern lobes.

The spore cases are initially
covered by curled-over lobe
edges. When they burst open,
spores fly out in all directions.

Spores

Young germinat-
ing sporophyte

Sperm

Archegonium

Gametophyte

Fertilization

Antheridium

Rhizoid

Mycelium

The fertilized ovum
grows into a sporophyte.

Sperm from the antheridium
swim to the archegonium.

The archegonium and
antheridium grow from the
gametophyte.

The spores grow into
heart-shaped gameto-
phytes called prothallia.

7

Astonishing Adapters

On the snowy slopes of Mount Cook in New Zealand, a tiny plant called the mountain crowfoot weathers the cold by manufacturing its own antifreeze. In the Arizona desert, meanwhile, the opuntia cactus reaches internal temperatures of 145° F. with no ill effects.

These hearty survivalists have mastered the skill of adaptation—the ability of an organism to tailor itself to its environment, no matter how harsh the conditions may be. As a plant adapts to an environment, it must adjust to climatic variables such as temperature and moisture, as well

as to biological stresses such as those brought on by predators.

Earth's history of environmental change is reflected not only in the adaptations of individual plants but also in the patterns of plant life worldwide. Drifting continents and ice ages have broadened the reach of some species—notably the miniature plants that grow on high mountains—and isolated others, such as the eucalyptus, which grows mainly in Australia.

Plants adapt to nature, but they also foster and sustain its delicate balance. As the source of the world's oxygen, they are the cornerstone of life on the planet. This chapter explores the marvelous and varied ways in which plants have evolved through the ages, as well as the role they play in maintaining the Earth's equilibrium.

Experts in the art of survival, the stone plant *(above, left)* camouflages itself, and the saguaro cactus *(above)* frightens off predators with its hard, spiny looks. Below, soil animals, fungi, and bacteria feed on the remains of dead plants, converting the matter into fertilizer.

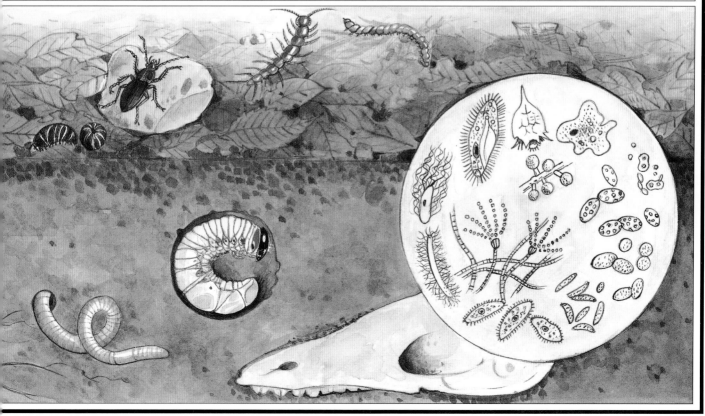

Why Does a Cactus Have Spines?

Hundreds of centuries ago, when deserts first started to spread across what is now the southwestern United States, the region's plants—until then accustomed to a moist, tropical environment—were threatened with extinction. Those that survived evolved some amazing mechanisms for dealing with the punishing heat and drought.

The most successful of these adaptations were made by the ancestor of the modern cactus, a small, leafy tree. Plants lose water through their leaves, so the small tree gave up its leaves and grew instead a network of spines *(below)* that shaded it from the sun, like a lattice screen. Water from desert fog or dew collected on the spines and trickled down to the plant's roots.

Transforming its leaves into spines was only one of the cactus's evolutionary tricks. To capture rain from rare cloudbursts, the cactus developed long, shallow roots that soak up water over a large area. The cactus also acquired spongy tissue in its stem for storing the collected water. In addition, many cacti evolved accordion-like ribs that allow their stems to expand when full of water and shrink when dry. Today, the stem of the largest cactus—the six-ton saguaro—holds as much as a ton of water, which swells its diameter by a foot. Other water-saving tactics are shown at right and below.

Broad-leaved cactus

Prickly pear cactus

Air-conditioned armor

The quill-shaped spines of a cactus *(right and below)* are specially adapted "leaves" that protect the plant from would-be predators—and keep it cool as well. Like small sunshades, the tufted spines scatter and reflect solar light, lowering the plant's surface temperature by as much as 20° F. The spines also trap an insulating layer of cooler air around the cactus that reduces heat absorption.

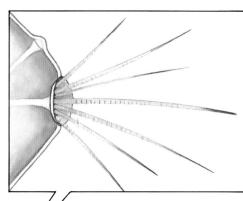

Spines grow from an areola.

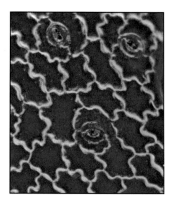

A cactus's stomas—surface pores used for "breathing"—close during the heat of the day to save water.

Like a tiny pincushion, the areola surrounds the spines, bristles, and hairs that grow from it.

The thick epidermis, or skin, has a waxy coating known as a cuticle, which prevents water loss.

The stem hoards water in its fleshy, spongy tissue; it also manufactures food for the cactus through photosynthesis.

Vascular bundles—tubular pathways running from the roots to the areolas—carry water and minerals through the cactus stem.

Prickly individuals

Most cacti—there are 1,500 species—belong to one of two groups. The branched category includes jointed cacti, such as prickly pears, which have segmented stems with many parts. The globular/columnar category includes the barrel cactus *(below, left)* and other cacti with ball-shaped stems, as well as the stately saguaro *(center)* and the hairy old-man cactus *(below, right)*.

Barrel cactus

Saguaro cactus

Old-man cactus

Building a better cactus

Early in their evolution, most cacti shed their leaves *(below)* in favor of heat-reflecting spines. Today's most advanced species have balloonlike stems with horny skins *(bottom)*.

Primitive cactus

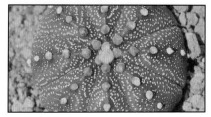

Advanced cactus

What Are Living Stones?

Hidden amid rock-strewn tablelands near Cape Town, South Africa, are millions of lithops—pebblelike plants that are often called living stones, or stone plants. Like the twig-shaped insect known as the walking stick, a stone plant bears an eerie resemblance to its surroundings. Most of the plant lies buried in the earth, but the tops of its exposed twin leaves are shaped and mottled like granite rocks, so the plant is easily overlooked by herbivores in search of food.

The stone plant's makeup brings other benefits, too. Its belowground dwelling place minimizes water loss by shielding the plant from the sun and drying winds. In addition, its camouflage coloring screens out direct sunlight: Dark markings on the leaves block incoming radiation, while semitransparent regions called windows admit solar energy to the buried plant. In this way, photosynthesis takes place while the plant avoids overexposure to the searing African sun.

New leaves grow each rainy season, when the stone plant's shallow roots sop up water from the flooded topsoil and transfer it to the spongy mesophyll for long-term storage *(right)*. As the old growth withers away, a single white or yellow bloom pushes up between the new leaves.

Inside a living stone

Two succulent leaves form the main body of a stone plant. The plant's anatomy, diagramed below, reflects its ingenious adaptation to a dry environment populated by thirsty plant eaters.

Cross section of a stone plant

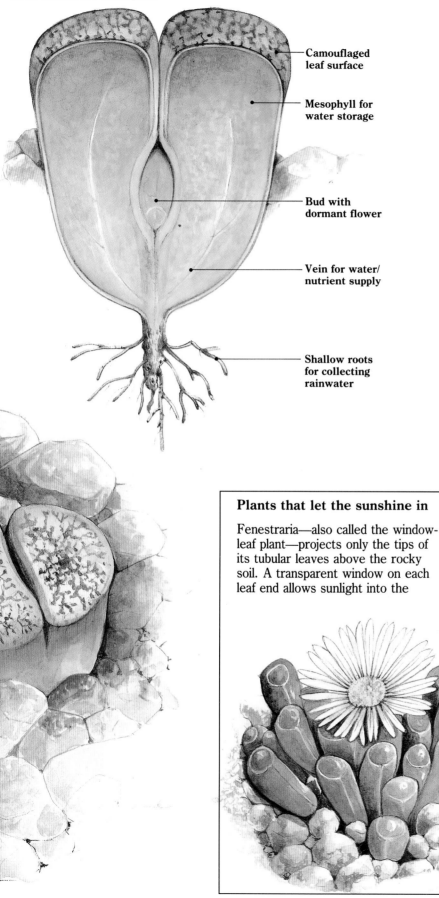

Camouflaged leaf surface

Mesophyll for water storage

Bud with dormant flower

Vein for water/ nutrient supply

Shallow roots for collecting rainwater

Daisies from stones

Seasonal rains spur the growth of a bud between the stone plant's leaves. The bud later blooms into a daisylike flower.

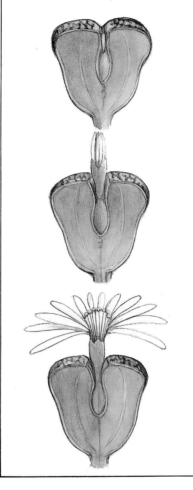

Plants that let the sunshine in

Fenestraria—also called the window-leaf plant—projects only the tips of its tubular leaves above the rocky soil. A transparent window on each leaf end allows sunlight into the plant's juicy interior, where photosynthetic cells use the energy to make food. Fenestraria is a close cousin of the stone plant; both inhabit the same arid region of Africa.

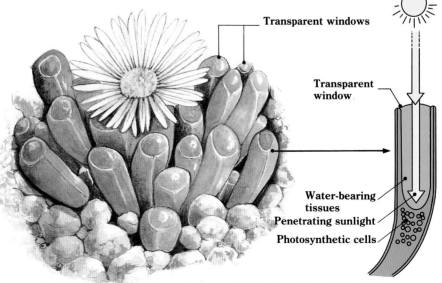

Transparent windows

Transparent window

Water-bearing tissues

Penetrating sunlight

Photosynthetic cells

Why Are Baobabs So Big?

One of the strangest plants in the world grows on the hot, dry savannas of Africa and Australia. It is the baobab *(right),* a barrel-shaped tree topped by a tangle of branches that are leafless except during the rainy season. The tallest baobabs reach a height of 75 feet, yet their diameter can range up to 85 feet.

The monstrous girth of the baobab helps it survive: The tree uses itself as a water reservoir. When it rains, the tree's corky tissues absorb water like a sponge, filling the partly hollow trunk with water. The baobab must ration its water carefully, so it grows very slowly. Some baobabs live to be 5,000 years old.

A baobab flower

A baobab fruit

The bounty of the baobab

Following the summer rains, the homely baobab enjoys a brief season of beauty. White blooms and velvety fruits *(above)* appear side by side on the tree's branches, which suddenly flourish with glossy leaves. The sweet-smelling flowers, 5 to 7 inches across, dangle upside down from willowy stalks. The mature fruits—about the length of a large banana and three times as wide—contain a seedy pulp that tastes like gingerbread; when dried and mixed with water, the pulp produces a refreshing "baobab lemonade." The seeds, fruits, and leaves can be eaten by people and animals. Fibers from the tree's thick bark make excellent fishnets, twine, and rough sacking for bags and coarse clothing.

A tourist inspects a 3,000-year-old baobab tree in western Australia. The tree, wider than it is tall, is one of several ancient baobabs growing in a preserve on the Kimberleys Plateau. Baobab trees are a protected species throughout Australia.

A leafless bottle tree heralds the coming dry season. A streamlined relative of the chunky baobab, the bottle tree sheds its leaves at the first sign of drought. The trunk—up to 60 feet across at the base—tapers slightly at the crown, giving the tree its distinctive cola-bottle shape.

Where Does Eucalyptus Grow?

Today, eucalyptus trees prosper in woodlands from Spain to India, along highways in California and Florida, and even in the dry reaches of South Africa. As recently as 1800, however, the trees could be found only in Australia, Tasmania, and New Guinea.

Eucalyptus trees were isolated on these three islands, some scientists believe, by events that occurred early in Earth's history. According to the theory of continental drift, the world's continents were once part of a single landmass, known as Pangaea *(opposite)*. Then, about 200 million years ago, forces deep within the Earth began to break the supercontinent apart. Australia drifted away from Pangaea, forming an island continent on which its native eucalyptus trees developed. The trees would not be spread around the globe until the 19th century, when eucalyptus saplings were exported to countries in need of the timber and shade provided by the fast-growing trees.

A koala delicacy

Eucalyptus trees make up 75 percent of Australia's forests. Their waxy, succulent leaves *(right)* are a favorite food of koalas *(left)*.

Eucalyptus leaves and flowers

Earth's floral regions

Continental drift and changes in climate have combined to produce six distinct floral regions worldwide *(right)*. Each region is classified according to the types of plants it contains. Many species found in the Holarctic region, for example, evolved from a common ancestor that thrived when the North American and Eurasian continents were still joined. Other plant species achieved a wide distribution thanks to the migrations of seed-carrying birds. Plants that are limited to one region—such as the eucalyptus— probably arose after the continents drifted apart.

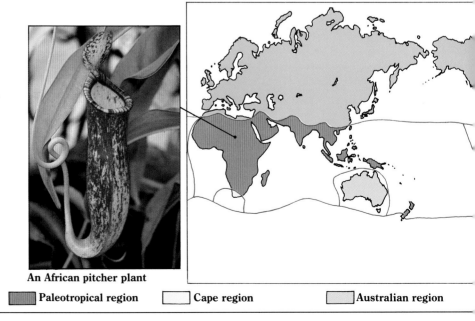

An African pitcher plant

| | Holarctic region | | Paleotropical region | | Cape region | | Australian region |

Variations on a green theme

Australia is home to nearly 500 species of eucalyptus trees. Forests of stately Sydney blue gums dominate the tropical north, while tiny snow gums and other frost-tolerant strains dot the mountains of the southeast. Drought-resistant species like the wandoo grow in the southern savanna. Only the west-central deserts support no eucalyptus trees.

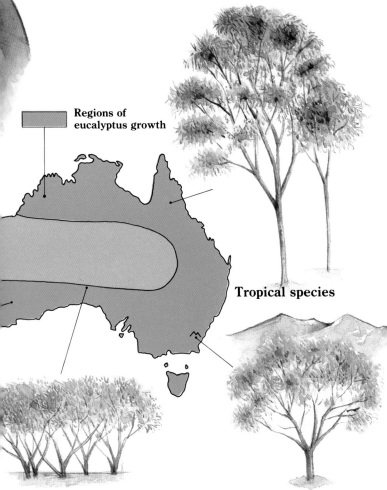

Regions of eucalyptus growth

Tropical species

Drought-resistant species

Frost-tolerant species

A South American water lily   A stand of Canadian larch

Neotropical region   Arctic region

The case of the creeping continents

Scholars noted the puzzlelike fit between the continents on either side of the Atlantic as early as the 17th century. In the 19th century, biologists discovered striking similarities in fossilized plants found in Europe and America, suggesting a common origin for both. Not until 1912, however—when German meteorologist Alfred Wegener proposed his theory of continental drift—did a few scientists begin to take seriously the idea that the continents had once been fused in a single landmass. Since then, scientists have used geologic, magnetic, and fossil evidence to reconstruct the location of the continents at various times in Earth's history; their best guesses are shown below.

200 million years ago

135 million years ago

65 million years ago

Today

How Have Alpine Plants Evolved?

High atop the world's mountains, above the line where evergreen forests give way to rocky meadows, lies a forbidding region known as the alpine zone. Here the air is thin, high winds scour the gravelly soil, and precipitation—when it comes—usually takes the form of snow.

By necessity, the plants that inhabit the alpine zone are some of the hardiest in the world. They probably first appeared there after the great ice age that began about 2 million years ago *(right)*. Before then, for a period of some 60 million years, the ancestors of these cold-loving plants grew on the tundra that surrounds the North Pole. As glaciers began to march south, however, the plants were forced to migrate toward the ice-free lower latitudes. Later, when the glaciers retreated, most of the tundra plants returned to their high-latitude soils, but some climbed to higher altitudes—the alpine zone—instead.

Today, the plants that live in the alpine zone have adapted remarkably well to their harsh environment. To minimize their exposure to gale-force winds near mountain summits, alpine plants lie low, forming dense, carpetlike mats on the frozen ground. Dwarf leaves cut heat and water loss, while extensive root systems anchor the plants in the stony soil. And because the summer growing season is so short—just 14 weeks in some places—the plants put forth showy blooms each spring to attract pollinators, transforming mountain meadows into a sea of brilliant colors.

1

Vertical vegetation zones

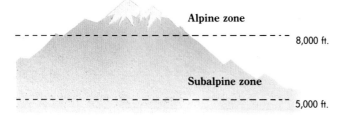

With increasing altitude, the trees on a mountainside slowly disappear. The transition point, known as the timberline, varies with latitude. On Japan's Chubu Mountains, for example, the timberline is 8,000 feet high. The alpine zone occupies the area between the timberline and the summit.

Summer flowers bloom in the alpine zone.

5

4

3

2

The diary of an ice age

1. Warmth. Tundra plants (flowers) and arctic trees (silver-green firs) inhabit high latitudes, while cold-climate evergreens (cone-shaped trees) populate the mountains. Temperate forests (round-topped trees) extend to lower latitudes.

2. Chill. Glaciers advance from the north, driving high-latitude flora south.

3. Glaciation. Hardy tundra plants rim the glacier, but both types of evergreen flee the snowbound mountains.

4. Thaw. As the glaciers recede, the tundra plants return to high latitudes; they also seek out high altitudes.

5. Warmth. Glacial retreat restores earlier floral patterns, but the tundra plants remain in their new alpine home.

Alpine plants and the ice ages

Plants flourishing in high mountain meadows owe their existence to the ice ages. Four times during the last two million years, vast ice sheets have advanced toward the equator from the poles *(above)*. As ice gripped the land, the grasses, lichens, and sedges that lived in the polar tundra were killed off. Their seeds, transported by birds and winds to the more hospitable lower latitudes, gave rise to a new community of polar plants.

As the Earth warmed and the glaciers retreated, however, the exiled tundra plants began to wither. Their seeds found their way back to their former polar neighborhood, where they again took root. Isolated pockets of tundra plants remained in the lower latitudes, however. These glacial refugees established themselves in the high mountains. They are the alpine plants of today.

Alpine adaptations

The alpine zone is a land of little precipitation, so many plants that grow there resemble desert plants. Edelweiss *(below, left)*, native to the Alps, has hairy, wax-coated leaves that seal in moisture. Its cousin, *Leontopodium fauriei (below, right)*, grows in Japan.

Edelweiss

Leontopodium fauriei

Which Tree Is the Largest?

In 1853, trappers returning from California told stories of trees big enough to hold an entire wagon train. No one believed their tall tales until a group of easterners went out west and found a redwood of such enormous girth that it took four men 22 days to fell it. Afterward, they turned the trunk into a double-lane bowling alley for gold prospectors.

History abounds with reports of such legendary trees, yet singling out one tree as the world's largest is probably impossible. A given tree, for example, may boast the world's thickest trunk while measuring tens of feet shorter than a lanky rival. Nonetheless, all of the trees shown here qualify as true giants.

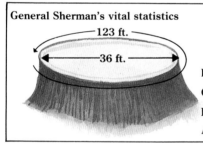

General Sherman's vital statistics

123 ft.

36 ft.

Diameter: 36 ft.

Circumference: 123 ft.

Height: 272 ft.

Age: 3,500 years

Giant sequoia

Sequoiadendron giganteum—literally "big tree"— is often cited as the world's largest tree species. The biggest (but not the tallest) of these California natives is named General Sherman; at 272 feet high and 36 feet in diameter, the tree contains enough lumber to build 80 five-room houses.

Sylvan skyscrapers

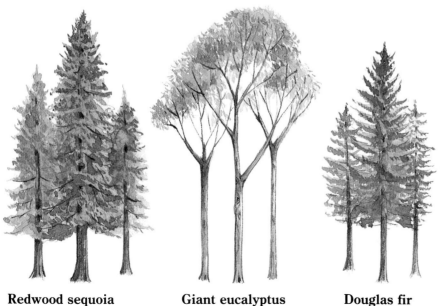

Redwood sequoia   **Giant eucalyptus**   **Douglas fir**

Among Earth's largest living things are three tree species so tall their tops seem to brush the roof of the sky: the redwood sequoia, the giant eucalyptus, and the Douglas fir. The tallest species —though only by a branch or so—is the redwood sequoia *(far left)*. The loftiest individual redwood, found in California's Coast Range, tops 394 feet. To reach these heights, redwoods require as much as 55 inches of rainfall a year. In second place at 374 feet is the giant eucalyptus *(center),* a species native to the southern forests of Australia and Tasmania. Its lightweight wood is often made into plywood and paper pulp. The ramrod-straight Douglas fir *(near left),* renowned for its hard timber, reaches 328 feet and grows in dense stands in the American Northwest. A single Douglas fir may be used as the tall mast of a sailing ship.

Kapok

Kauri pine

The kapok, or ceiba, tree supports its massive trunk with buttresses that stretch 30 feet beyond its base, which measures 160 feet in diameter. The kapok tree yields fruits whose seeds sport a fleecy covering used in pillows, sleeping bags, life preservers, and soundproofing insulation.

Like a Roman column, the kauri pine measures the same at its base—about 20 feet across—as it does below its first branch, some 80 feet off the ground. This majestic tree, coveted for its valuable wood, has been logged almost to extinction in its native New Zealand.

A bristlecone pine in California

The old ones

The world's largest trees are also often the oldest. Japan's Jomon cedar, whose trunk is more than 90 feet in circumference, has been alive for at least 3,000 years. Some sequoias and ceibas are between 3,000 and 5,000 years old. But the bristlecone pine *(left),* the grandfather of them all, rarely grows more than 25 feet tall. A stunted and gnarled plant, it flourishes on the wind-swept, rock-strewn slopes of the White Mountains near the California-Nevada border. The oldest known bristlecone pine is the Methuselah Tree; more than 4,600 years old, it was already a sapling when the Egyptians started building the pyramids.

Gauging the age of ancient trees is a complex and inexact science. Carbon dating, the most commonly used method, measures the half-life of radioactive carbon present in tree fiber as an age index. A simpler approach is to count the yearly growth rings in a core sample taken from the trunk of the tree.

What Is the Food Chain?

Energy and matter are constantly recycled in the zone of air, water, and land called the biosphere. Through photosynthesis, plants convert energy from the sun into fuel for growth. These organisms make their own food, so they are called producers. Other living things—crickets and humans, for example—cannot manufacture food from sunlight. Instead, they must eat other organisms to obtain the energy that keeps them alive. This group of creatures is therefore labeled consumers *(far right)*.

Directly or indirectly, all consumers derive their nourishment from plants—either by eating plants themselves or by eating other creatures who eat plants. In this sense, plants are the very foundation of life. The term for this plant-based life cycle is the food chain.

The final link in the chain is made up of decomposers—that is, organisms like bacteria and fungi that break down the dead remains of producers and consumers, returning energy-packed nutrients to the soil for plant use.

The food chain helps maintain the balance of nature. During photosynthesis, producers take in water and carbon dioxide and give off oxygen. Consumers and decomposers, by contrast, absorb oxygen and emit carbon dioxide. Through this give-and-take, the two gases remain at their proper concentrations in the atmosphere.

Through photosynthesis, plants produce food for themselves; they also become food for the world.

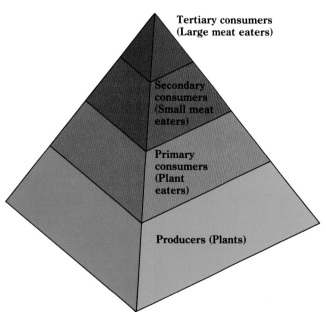

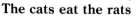

The cats eat the rats

The relationships and relative populations of each group in the food chain are shown above. Plants, whose energy source is the sun, are the most numerous; tertiary consumers—large animals who eat smaller animals that eat other creatures who eat plants—number the fewest.

Tracing energy's path

Solar energy

The food cycle begins as plants use solar energy *(left)* to manufacture tissues. These producers become food for primary consumers—herbivores such as grasshoppers and giraffes. Primary consumers are in turn devoured by meat-eating sec- ondary consumers like snakes and hyenas. Still- larger carnivores, known as tertiary consumers, then prey on secondary consumers. In practice, consumers move between levels, creating an in- tricate energy exchange known as the food chain.

Plants: the basis of life

The energy that fuels Earth's life cycles comes from the sun. But only green plants can make direct use of this energy source. They are equipped with photosynthetic cells, which convert sunlight into chemical energy for building new tissue. Without the unique ability of plants to exploit solar energy in this way, other creatures would have no food.

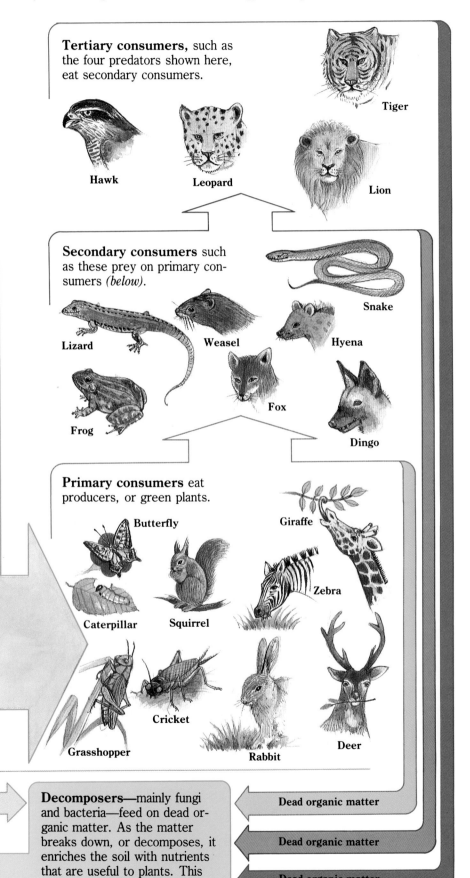

Tertiary consumers, such as the four predators shown here, eat secondary consumers.

Hawk

Leopard

Tiger

Lion

Secondary consumers such as these prey on primary con- sumers *(below).*

Lizard

Weasel

Snake

Hyena

Frog

Fox

Dingo

Primary consumers eat producers, or green plants.

Butterfly

Giraffe

Caterpillar

Squirrel

Zebra

Grasshopper

Cricket

Rabbit

Deer

Flowers, nectar, leaves

Sap

Grass

Decaying plant matter

Minerals

Decomposers—mainly fungi and bacteria—feed on dead or- ganic matter. As the matter breaks down, or decomposes, it enriches the soil with nutrients that are useful to plants. This completes the food cycle.

Dead organic matter

Dead organic matter

Dead organic matter

What Happens to Fallen Leaves?

Billions of leaves fall in woodlands around the world each year, yet the leaf pile on the forest floor never grows any deeper. That's because it never really gets the chance: Legions of largely unseen organisms begin consuming the fallen leaves as soon as they dry and crumble.

First at the feast are bacteria, mildew, and decomposer fungi *(near right)*, which use digestive enzymes to break down the leaf tissue. The partly decomposed leaves are then eaten by earthworms and other tiny animals *(far right)*. Gnawing and chewing, these creatures reduce the moldering leaves to a fine dust; in the process, they excrete a rich store of digested wastes. The droppings and leaf dust then become a second course for the bacteria and fungi. Together these sources of food are so bountiful that a handful of forest dirt contains as many organisms as there are people on Earth.

The end result is that leaves and other dead organic matter are broken down into simpler substances—chiefly proteins and minerals—that are reabsorbed by living plants. The network of soil animals, bacteria, and fungi that performs this recycling is known as the saprophytic chain. The time required to complete the chain depends on the temperature and humidity of the soil and the composition of the leaves. Under normal conditions in a temperate forest, the fragile tissues of a deciduous leaf decompose within a year. The waxy, compact needles of an evergreen, however, resist the forces of decay for years.

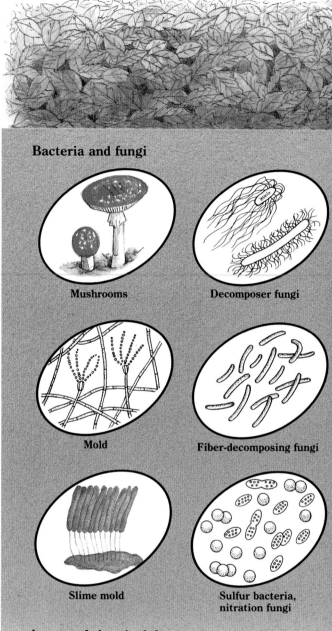

Bacteria and fungi

Mushrooms

Decomposer fungi

Mold

Fiber-decomposing fungi

Slime mold

Sulfur bacteria, nitration fungi

Agents of chemical decay

Decay-producing fungi and bacteria *(above)* secrete chemical enzymes that break down proteins and carbohydrates found in animal droppings and tissues, and in rotting plant matter. The organisms then absorb the soluble nutrients in the digested material, leaving behind decomposed organic matter as soil fertilizer.

Leaf factories

Fallen leaves are a big part of the decomposers' diet. The most prolific producers of leaf fall are broad-leaved, deciduous forests in regions of marked seasonal change. Here the cooler, shorter days of autumn slow sap flow, causing the trees to shed their leaves. Trees in the monsoon forests of Indochina also drop their leaves all at once, during the annual dry season. Others, such as northern evergreen-needle-leaf forests and tropical evergreen-broadleaf forests, lose their leaves continuously.

Autumn leaves carpet a forest floor.

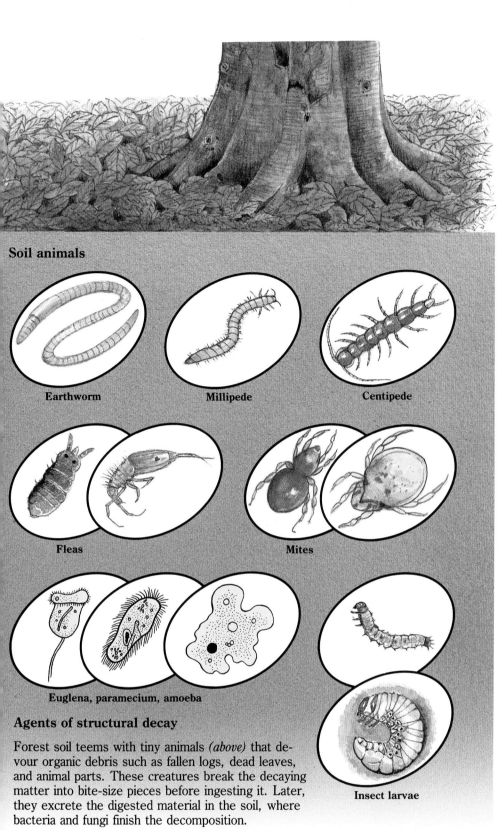

Soil animals

Earthworm

Millipede

Centipede

Fleas

Mites

Euglena, paramecium, amoeba

Insect larvae

Agents of structural decay

Forest soil teems with tiny animals *(above)* that devour organic debris such as fallen logs, dead leaves, and animal parts. These creatures break the decaying matter into bite-size pieces before ingesting it. Later, they excrete the digested material in the soil, where bacteria and fungi finish the decomposition.

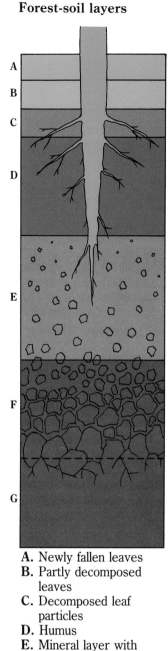

Forest-soil layers

A
B
C
D
E
F
G

A. Newly fallen leaves
B. Partly decomposed leaves
C. Decomposed leaf particles
D. Humus
E. Mineral layer with scattered humus
F. Weathered rock and stone
G. Bedrock

Humus: recycled plant food

Fungi, bacteria, and a host of soil animals work together to convert leaf litter, twigs, and other organic refuse into the moist black substance known as humus. A tossed salad of proteins and lignin (a constituent of wood), humus is an essential ingredient of good growing soil. In addition to furnishing vital nutrients, it boosts the ability of soil to retain water. Most important, humus aids in the formation of soil crumbs—tiny clumped particles that create air spaces in the soil. Soil organisms draw oxygen into these air spaces, fostering plant growth.

Such benefits extend only 3 feet or so beneath the forest floor, however. As illustrated above, humus is concentrated in a fairly thin band of topsoil below a layered blanket of decaying leaves. Underneath the humus is a hard-packed mineral layer; below this lie layers of unyielding rock.

Can a Lake Turn Into a Forest?

Like mountains, lakes seem to be fixed features of the landscape, yet they too are subject to change. Under certain conditions, a lake can become a woodland in just a few thousand years.

The best candidate for such a transformation is a river-fed mountain lake. Over hundreds of years, the river deposits tons of sediment into the lake, filling in the shoreline and raising the lake bottom. Water plants soon colonize the shallows near the shore. As sediment raises the lake bed still higher, plants such as water lilies, reeds, and ditch grass fill in the open areas. The lake becomes a marsh.

Rotting plants then accumulate below the dense marsh growth, where they turn into an organic muck known as peat. Cattails, sphagnum moss, and bulrushes sprout on the peat. The marsh becomes a swamp.

Among the new swamp dwellers are alders and willows; these water-loving trees convert the swamp into a meadow. Birches, red pines, and other sun trees—species that thrive on full sun—spring up, forming a fledgling wood. Finally, shade trees appear and the wood matures into a climax forest—that is, a stable community of trees. This process of change, in which one plant community replaces another until equilibrium is reached, is called succession.

A tale of two bogs

Low-lying swamps flushed by running water develop into low-moor bogs *(right)*. In these wetlands, dead plant matter decays and is swept away before it can form layers of peat. The water flow also washes minerals away from growing ditch reeds and rushes, depriving them of nutrients. Thus low-moor bogs support little plant life.

High-moor bogs *(lower right)* form on flooded plains in regions where the air is consistently chill and damp. Such bogs favor the growth of sphagnum moss—tiny, spongelike plants that gather in tufts. As new growth develops, the underlying moss withers and turns to peat. Over years, the peat swells into a dense mound that rises above the plain.

Tiny lakes dot a high-moor bog in Ozegahara, Japan.

Mounting sediment reduces the lake's depth. The plants migrate inward.

The water plants close in on the lake's center, turning the lake to marsh.

As dead plant matter accumulates, it forms a swamp that hosts ditch reeds and sedge.

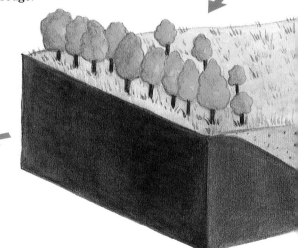

Alders and other water-loving trees occupy a swampy meadow. A sun-tree forest soon grows up, creating a leafy canopy under which shade-tolerant trees can flourish. In time, a climax forest of oak and hickory develops.

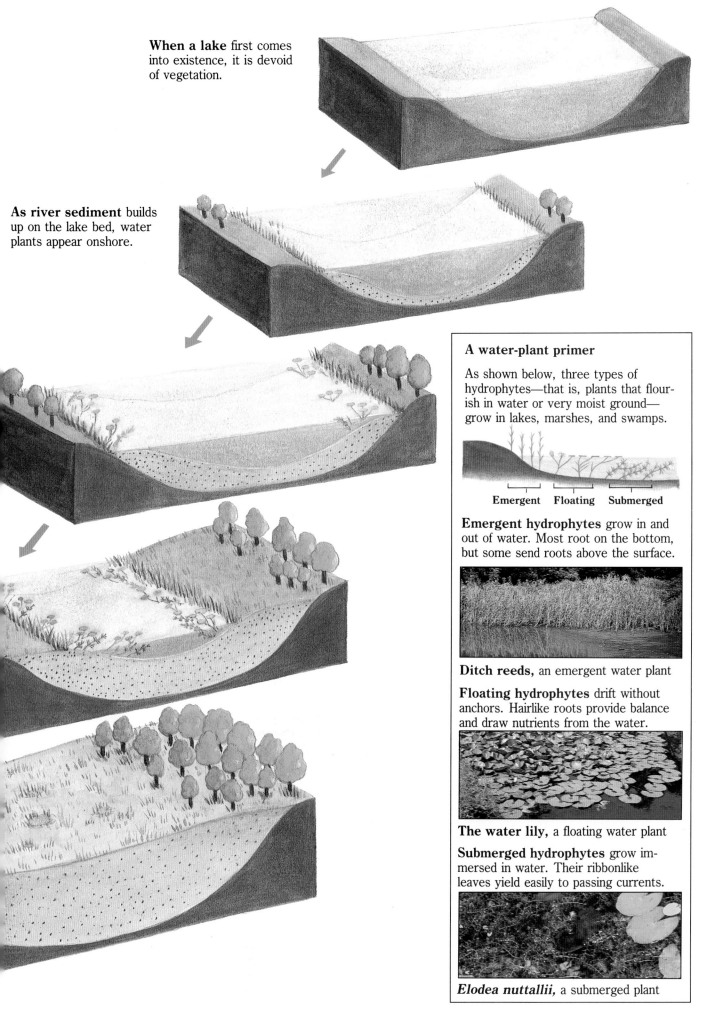

When a lake first comes into existence, it is devoid of vegetation.

As river sediment builds up on the lake bed, water plants appear onshore.

A water-plant primer

As shown below, three types of hydrophytes—that is, plants that flourish in water or very moist ground—grow in lakes, marshes, and swamps.

Emergent   Floating   Submerged

Emergent hydrophytes grow in and out of water. Most root on the bottom, but some send roots above the surface.

Ditch reeds, an emergent water plant

Floating hydrophytes drift without anchors. Hairlike roots provide balance and draw nutrients from the water.

The water lily, a floating water plant

Submerged hydrophytes grow immersed in water. Their ribbonlike leaves yield easily to passing currents.

Elodea nuttallii, a submerged plant

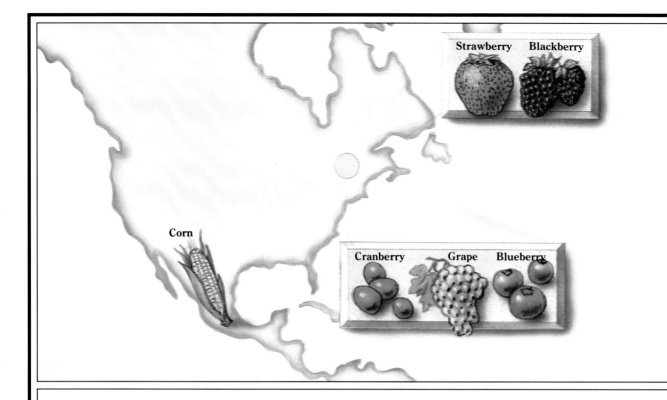

8

The Human Connection

Our early ancestors were hunters and gatherers of wild plants for food. When they began to save seeds and sow them, the hunter-gatherers became farmers, and different wild plants became their staple food crops. In southwestern Asia, wild grasses became barley and wheat. In tropical America, wild corn, squashes, beans, peppers, potatoes, and peanuts emerged as the favored plants. Over the millennia, farmers gradually improved these crops by the simple expedient of saving the most productive or pre-

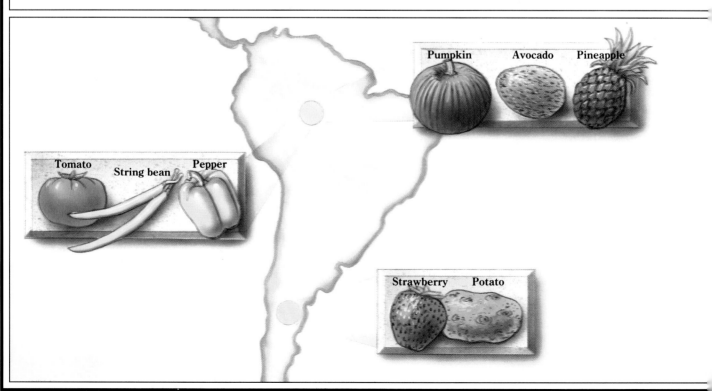

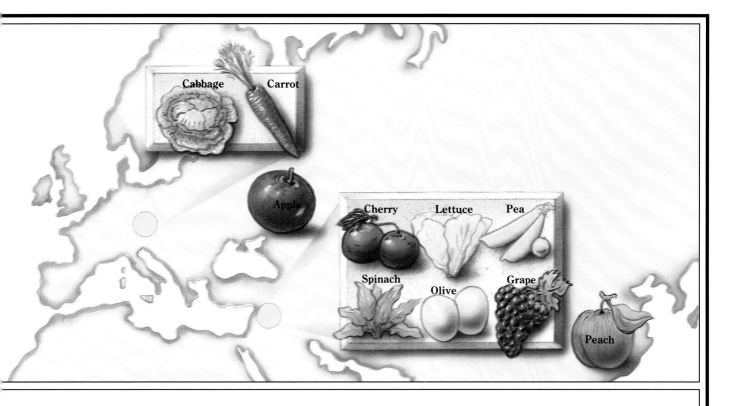

ferred kinds for replanting the next year; in this way, wild plants began their lengthy transformation into the advanced crops that feed the world.

Today, the challenge is to conserve not only the wild progenitors of plants but also the primitive land races—the crop strains that have been passed from one generation of farmers to the next. The application of these plant genetic resources, as they are called, will continue to be a busy field of research in which scientists try to transfer single genes from one plant to another,

or to use genes from distant relatives of tame crops. Along with current crop-improvement technology, such advances will be essential to feeding the world's exploding population.

Civilization could not have advanced without the movement of crop progenitors from the areas where they originated *(maps, above and below)* to the population centers of the world. The discovery of the Americas enriched the world's food diversity with more than 10 crop plants of worldwide importance.

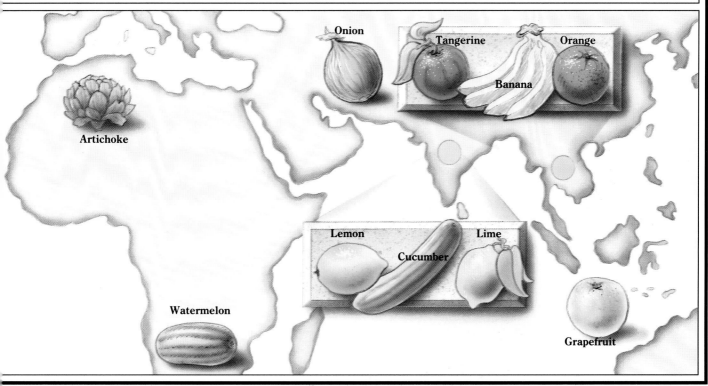

Which Medicines Come from Plants?

Before synthetic drugs were developed in the 20th century, nearly all medicines—from folk remedies to pure chemical compounds—were derived from plants. Today, 40 percent of the prescription drugs sold in the United States still contain at least one ingredient taken from plants. Extracts from the common ground cover known as periwinkle, for example, are used to battle several kinds of cancer, including leukemia. Preparations from the foxglove—an ornamental flower—are effective in treating heart disease. Another flower, the opium poppy, is the source of the painkiller morphine. In addition to investigating known plants, researchers are combing the globe in the hope of discovering new species with medicinal properties.

Some of the most potent medicines come from some of nature's lowliest plants—fungi. Known as antibiotics (from the Greek words meaning "against life"), these substances cure illness by preventing the growth of other living cells, such as bacteria. Penicillin, the first known antibiotic, was discovered by British bacteriologist Sir Alexander Fleming in 1928. Since then, scientists have found dozens of other naturally occurring antibiotics. Their quest continues today.

The pioneers of penicillin

Penicillin, discovered by Sir Alexander Fleming *(below)* in 1928, was refined into an effective bacteria-fighting drug in 1941 by British scientists Howard Florey and Ernst Chain. In 1945 the three men were awarded the Nobel Prize for their invaluable contribution to medicine.

From mold to medicine

An antibiotic is a chemical substance, produced by microorganisms such as fungi and bacteria, that stops or destroys other microorganisms. Penicillin, for example, is manufactured naturally by mold fungi of the *Penicillium* genus. It is used to fight a variety of bacterial diseases, from ear infections to pneumonia, scarlet fever, and meningitis.

Not all types of bacteria are harmful to human health, however. The order of bacteria known as Actinomycetales yields several potent antibiotics, notably streptomycin. Isolated in molds by the Russian-born American microbiologist Selman Waksman in 1943, streptomycin has been successful in fighting tuberculosis and other bacterial diseases.

In the years since antibiotics were introduced, however, certain bacteria have developed a resistance to some drugs. To combat these stubborn strains, doctors often prescribe a mix of two or more antibiotics. Meanwhile, scientists continue to search for new antibiotics.

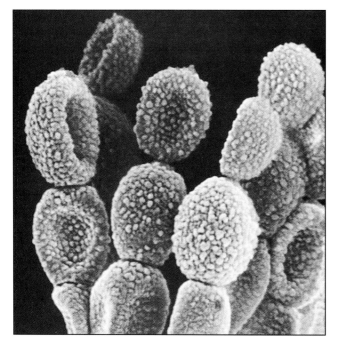

Fuzzy spores grow on blue mold, the source of penicillin.

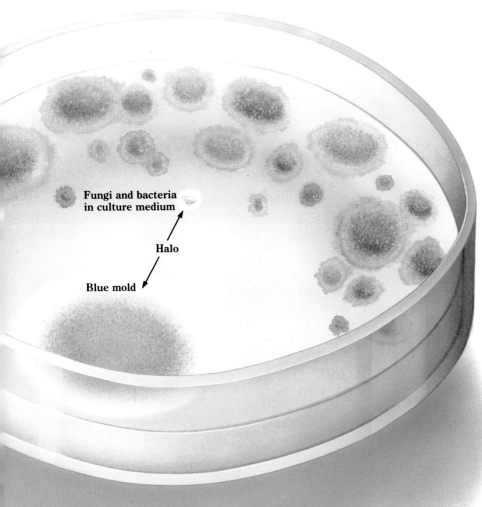

Fungi and bacteria
in culture medium

Halo

Blue mold

Viewed through an electron microscope, blue mold is revealed to be a tiny plant with long stalks.

Shown below is a blue-mold colony of the type that produces penicillin. The colony is ringed by its bacteria-fighting halo.

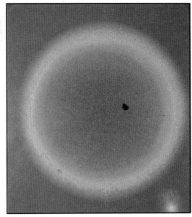

Mysterious molds with halos

While studying the bacterium *Staphylococcus* in 1928, Alexander Fleming noticed that a blue mold had invaded the culture medium. Surrounding the mold was an open space, later termed a halo, in which no bacteria grew *(above)*. The blue mold, Fleming concluded, produced a chemical substance that halted bacterial growth. He later named this chemical *penicillin* because the blue mold belongs to the *Penicillium* genus.

An antibiotic treasure-trove

The genus of bacteria known as *Streptomyces* has proved to be a rich source of antibiotics. Among them are antibacterial drugs such as streptomycin, useful in treating tuberculosis, and tetracycline, which effectively fights a broad spectrum of bacteria. *Erythraeus,* a species of *Streptomyces,* yields erythromycin, a popular treatment for bacterial illnesses such as strep throat, legionnaires' disease, and some pneumonias. Certain *Streptomyces* antibiotics, in combination with other drugs, can even help to slow down the growth of cancer.

The lesser strains

Outside of the *Penicillium* and *Streptomyces* genuses, only a few fungi and bacteria produce antibiotics. The drug polymyxin, for example, which works against whooping cough, is obtained from a soil bacterium of the *Bacillus* genus. Another strain of *Bacillus* yields the antibiotic called bacitracin, revered by teenagers for its effectiveness in fighting bacterial skin infections.

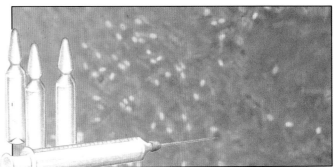

Bacillus bacteria when magnified

What Is Grafting?

Nursery workers and gardeners use an array of techniques to propagate herbs and woody plants by vegetative means—that is, without the need for sexual reproduction. The most widespread and least expensive such method is the use of cuttings. When propagation by cutting does not succeed, an alternative approach such as layering, dividing, or grafting plants may be used instead.

Grafting is one of the oldest ways to achieve vegetative propagation; plant breeders have practiced the tactic for more than 2,000 years. In essence, the gardener unites parts of two closely related plants so that a piece of a desirable plant starts to grow on the roots of the second plant. The plant to be reproduced is called the scion, while the rooted plant is known as the stock.

Grafting serves many purposes. First, it enables a grower to change the character of a plant by modifying its wood, foliage, or fruit. Second, it permits the development of branches, flowers, or fruit on trees or shrubs that lack them. Third, grafting is a good way to enhance the vigor of defective or exhausted trees or shrubs. Fourth, it facilitates the reproduction of dioecious—that is, separate-sex—plants, since a scion of one sex can be grafted onto a stock of the opposite sex. And finally, grafting offers botanists and other scientists a means to preserve and reproduce varieties of woody and herbaceous plants when other techniques fail.

The basics of grafting

Although woody plants may be grafted in any month, the operation has a higher chance of success at certain times of the year. Periods of intense cambial activity are ideal. In early spring, for example, the tree buds swell and the wounds made by grafting heal most rapidly. A second period of cambial activity extends from midsummer into early fall. Root grafting is performed indoors in late winter, when the root pieces are dormant. Several grafting techniques are illustrated on these pages.

Notch grafting

Crown, or notch, grafting *(below)* is often used to produce dwarf fruit trees. The new tree that results from the graft will duplicate the features of the scion, but its growth rate will be dictated by the rootstock.

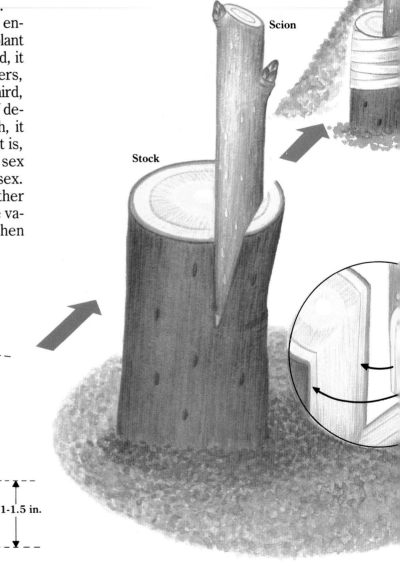

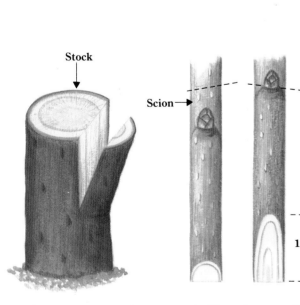

1. To begin, the stock is cut off square; a sharp, sterile knife is used to make a downward V-shaped groove.

2. The scion, usually containing a total of three buds, is cut in the shape of a wedge and inserted snugly into the notch.

3. The surfaces of both the scion and the stock must be cut cleanly; their cambiums must also be aligned to bring them into close contact.

5. The sprouting of a bud *(below)* signals that the graft has taken. The soil can now be removed; the tape will have disintegrated already *(right)*.

4. The union is secured with grafting tape *(left)*. To keep the graft from drying out, all cut surfaces are covered with grafting wax or mounded soil.

Cleft grafting

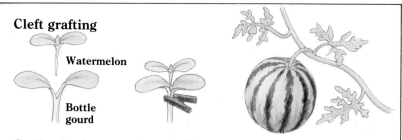

Watermelon

Bottle gourd

Grafting is often experimental. Here, a wedge-shaped scion from a watermelon has been inserted into a cleft in a disease-resistant bottle gourd and clamped in place.

Inarching

Inarching is used with ornamental trees. A potted seedling is placed beside the donor plant. Bark is sliced from adjacent sides of each plant, and the cut surfaces are joined. After the graft unites, the new plant (the one in the pot) is cut free above and below the union.

Budding

To propagate a rose, a lilac, or a fruit tree by budding, the scion—here, a wood sliver with one bud—is inserted beneath the bark of the stock and tied with rubber budding strips.

Root grafting

Root grafting, in which the stock is a seedling or a pencil-size piece of dormant root, takes place in winter. The grafted plants are buried in moist sand in cold storage; they are transplanted in early spring.

Posies from a potato

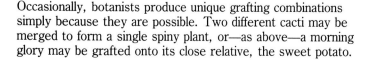

Occasionally, botanists produce unique grafting combinations simply because they are possible. Two different cacti may be merged to form a single spiny plant, or—as above—a morning glory may be grafted onto its close relative, the sweet potato.

How Are Hybrids Produced?

When two genetically similar plants—such as two closely related species or varieties of tomato—are crossbred, their offspring are known as hybrids. In general, hybrids outperform their parents in growth, yield, and vigor. This phenomenon, known as hybrid vigor or heterosis, has long influenced cultivation, as farmers tried more or less haphazardly to improve their crops through random crosses and mass selection. Early in the 20th century, however, the infant science of genetics revealed that traits are passed from one generation of plants to the next by genes. This finding enabled humans to closely control the hybridization process.

The superior offspring that result from crossing two varieties of the same plant species are called F_1 hybrids. But F_1 hybrids do not breed true; when their seeds are sown, the next generation (F_2) is uneven in quality. To ensure the consistency of F_1 hybrids, the parental lines must be crossed every year to obtain new seeds.

Applying their knowledge of genetics, modern plant breeders are developing hybrids with various desirable traits—resistance to disease, for example, or a tendency to produce sweeter fruit. The basic process involves selecting promising parent plants, crossing them, and growing the resulting seeds. Because breeders usually raise several generations by backcrossing and grow thousands of seedlings before narrowing the selection to a promising few, producing a superior hybrid can consume more than a decade.

Breeding the best corn

Because corn is normally cross-fertilized, it offers a good example of the harmful effects of inbreeding. When a high-yielding strain is repeatedly self-fertilized, it loses vigor, yield, and quality because of its genetic isolation.

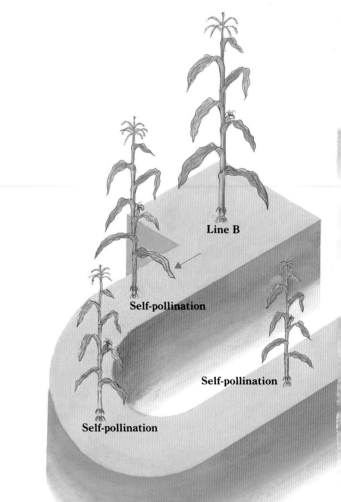

Line B

Self-pollination

Self-pollination

Self-pollination

A wealth of hybrids

Food stores and markets overflow with hybrid fruits and vegetables. Many widely available strawberries, tomatoes, green peppers, onions, and types of spinach are hybrids.

Growers favor hybrids for many reasons. Because they are bred to resist disease, pests, and drought, hybrids generally yield bigger and better crops. Hybrids also are uniform and produce handsomer, tastier, and less perishable versions of many fruits and vegetables.

Tomato   Green pepper   Spinach

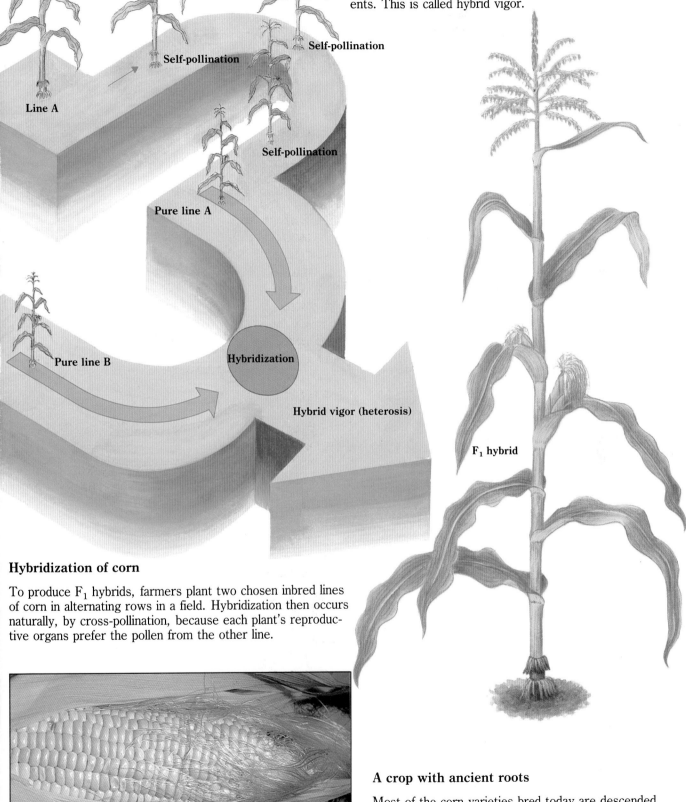

The path to F_1 corn

After a strain of corn has self-pollinated for several generations, a pure parental line with selected traits is produced. Along the way, the individual plants become smaller and the crop itself decreases, a phenomenon known as inbreeding depression. However, crossing two inbred lines *(A and B, left)* results in vigorous F_1 progeny *(below)*, which combine the best qualities of both parents. This is called hybrid vigor.

Self-pollination

Self-pollination

Line A

Self-pollination

Self-pollination

Pure line A

Hybridization

Pure line B

Hybrid vigor (heterosis)

F_1 hybrid

Hybridization of corn

To produce F_1 hybrids, farmers plant two chosen inbred lines of corn in alternating rows in a field. Hybridization then occurs naturally, by cross-pollination, because each plant's reproductive organs prefer the pollen from the other line.

A crop with ancient roots

Most of the corn varieties bred today are descended from a wild maize that grew in Mexico more than 7,000 years ago. Feed corn for cattle and the sweet corn eaten by people are almost always hybrid varieties.

Sweet corn, an F_1 hybrid, is packed with juicy kernels.

What Is Crop Improvement?

For as long as humans have cultivated plants, they have sought to improve them—that is, to enhance a crop's yield or quality or both. The earliest method of crop improvement, mass selection, consisted of choosing individual plants that exhibited the best traits and saving their seeds to sow the following year.

Occasionally, growers found among their crops a plant or two that differed radically from their parents. These odd offspring—now known as mutations—resulted from a sudden and random change in some hereditary, or genetic, characteristic. Although most mutations are defective, a rare few display positive traits that actually improve a plant line. Mutation breeding is just one of many crop-improvement methods that modern plant breeders are using with success.

Breeding breakthroughs

Increased understanding of genetics has taken much of the guesswork out of plant breeding. Knowledge of dominant and recessive traits, for instance, helps scientists predict the results of crossbreeding *(pages 136-137)*, a process that has yielded many of the rice and wheat varieties grown around the world.

Other methods manipulate crops at the gene level. Genes, which are carried in the nuclei of plant cells on tiny threads called chromosomes, determine heredity. In mutation breeding *(right, top)*, scientists use radiation to cause gene mutation; they then select the most promising specimens for future cultivation and refinement. Polyploidic breeding *(right, bottom)* hinges on the use of chemicals to multiply the number of chromosomes in a plant. The resulting polyploids, as they are termed, generally grow larger than normal plants.

When sets of chromosomes from two or more different species are combined—a method known as interspecific breeding—the result is an entirely new species of plant. The newcomer tends to be sterile, but its fertility may be restored by multiplying its chromosomes. Breeding methods that operate at the cellular and genetic levels are often referred to as biotechnology or genetic engineering.

Mutation by radiation

Although natural mutations occur very rarely, they can be brought about artificially by agents known as mutagens. X-rays, ultraviolet light, atomic radiation, and certain chemicals can all increase the mutation rate.

Most of the mutants that result from exposure to such agents are defective or lack commercial value. A few, however, display the sort of traits that breeders value: The nectarine, for example, is a bud mutation of the peach.

In general, the probability of mutation increases with the radiation dosage. (Although the level of radiation used is harmless to consumers of the crop, too much radiation will cause all the plants to die.) In a gamma field, shown at right, plants are grown around a platform containing cobalt 60, a radioactive isotope that emits gamma rays. The radiation bath may produce a hardier strain of rice, for instance, or a mulberry tree whose leaves are an unusual yellow color.

Polyploidic breeding

Most plants are diploid, or 2n, meaning that they have two sets of chromosomes. On occasion, however, the chromosomes in a reproductive cell fail to separate as usual, and fertilization results in offspring with three (triploid, 3n) or four (tetraploid, 4n) sets of chromosomes. These so-called polyploids, which occur spontaneously in nature, produce abnormally large flowers and fruits.

In 1937 an American scientist named Albert Blakeslee discovered that the chemical colchicine, an extract of the autumn crocus, multiplied the chromosome number of plant cells and prevented cell division from occurring. Because triploids and other odd-numbered polyploids often turn out to be sterile, botanists have used Blakeslee's discovery to produce such fruits as seedless watermelons.

Blue daisy tetraploids

Diploid seeds (2n)

Seedless melons

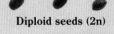

Diploids (2n→4n)

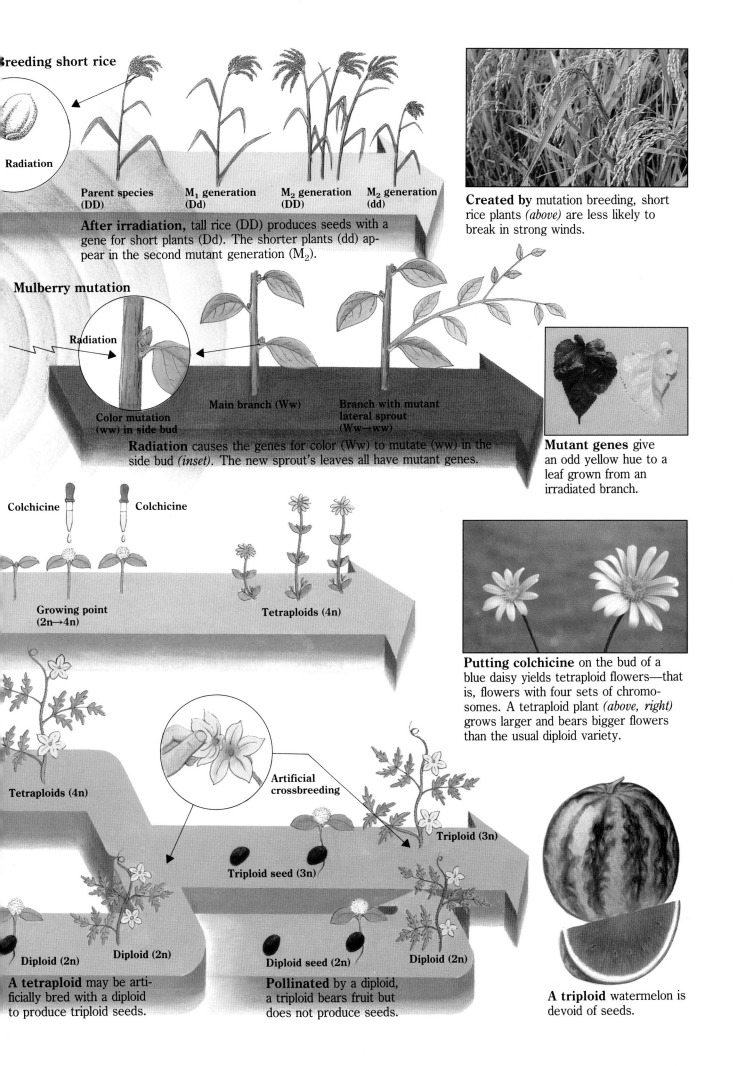

Breeding short rice

Radiation

Parent species
(DD)

M₁ generation
(Dd)

M₂ generation
(DD)

M₂ generation
(dd)

After irradiation, tall rice (DD) produces seeds with a gene for short plants (Dd). The shorter plants (dd) appear in the second mutant generation (M₂).

Created by mutation breeding, short rice plants *(above)* are less likely to break in strong winds.

Mulberry mutation

Radiation

Color mutation
(ww) in side bud

Main branch (Ww)

Branch with mutant
lateral sprout
(Ww→ww)

Radiation causes the genes for color (Ww) to mutate (ww) in the side bud *(inset).* The new sprout's leaves all have mutant genes.

Mutant genes give an odd yellow hue to a leaf grown from an irradiated branch.

Colchicine

Colchicine

Growing point
(2n→4n)

Tetraploids (4n)

Putting colchicine on the bud of a blue daisy yields tetraploid flowers—that is, flowers with four sets of chromosomes. A tetraploid plant *(above, right)* grows larger and bears bigger flowers than the usual diploid variety.

Tetraploids (4n)

Artificial
crossbreeding

Triploid (3n)

Triploid seed (3n)

Diploid (2n)

Diploid (2n)

Diploid seed (2n)

Diploid (2n)

A tetraploid may be artificially bred with a diploid to produce triploid seeds.

Pollinated by a diploid, a triploid bears fruit but does not produce seeds.

A triploid watermelon is devoid of seeds.

Can Plants Be Grown in Test Tubes?

Tissue culture—growing a plant in a test tube—is an artificial means of propagation, but the technique depends on a natural process: the capacity of plants to regenerate, or replace, a lost or damaged body part with new growth. First, a small piece of plant tissue is isolated in a sterilized environment such as a test tube. The tissue is then nourished with a suitable growth medium. Given the proper conditions, an entire plant can be regenerated from a tiny bit of tissue, or even from a single cell.

Tissue culture is most successful when the samples to be regenerated come from a plant's meristems—areas such as the growing tips of stems and roots, where cells are actively dividing. This type of propagation, called meristem culture or shoot-tip culture, produces plantlets that are genetically identical to the parent. Shoot-tip culture is often used to propagate seedless plants or F_1 hybrids.

Plant breeders prize meristem culture because it results in virus-free stock: The growing tips used to produce the new plants are generally free of viral infections, which tend to pass from one generation to the next when seedlings are produced by natural propagation or grafting. Meristem culture is also favored because it yields a large quantity of healthy, uniform plantlets in a short time.

Growing orchids in vitro

As a first step in tissue culture, a bud is sliced from the stem of an orchid *(left)*. A microscopic speck of tissue is then removed from the bud *(center inset)* and placed in a liquid growth medium *(above)*. About two months later, an organ called a globe appears in the test tube.

The cattleya orchid *(opposite, top)* is often grown by tissue culture *(above and right)* in a sterilized room, with the containers kept closed whenever possible to keep out germs. The growth medium contains all the nutrients and hormones needed to sustain the plant.

Variations on a theme

Shoot-tip culture *(above)* is not the only way to grow plants artificially. Callus culture, for example, can be used to reproduce herbs such as gromwell *(below)* and ginseng. Formed at the wounded surface of a plant or its root, callus tissue is composed of actively multiplying cells; it is therefore an ideal candidate for test-tube, or in vitro, propagation.

Two other major types of in vitro cultivation are embryo culture *(right, top)* and anther culture *(right, bottom)*. Regardless of the technique, tissue culture is always performed in an antiseptic environment where temperature, humidity, light, and other conditions can be carefully controlled.

Embryo culture is used in cases where fertilization has been successful but the embryo is likely to die if left on the plant. Hybrid lilies are produced by this method.

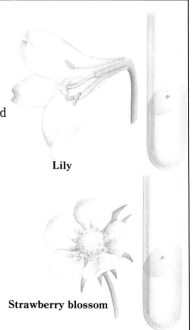

Lily

Strawberries and tobacco are among the plants that can be grown by anther culture—the cultivation of the anther, or the pollen-bearing part of a plant's stamen.

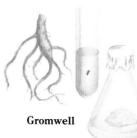

Gromwell

Strawberry blossom

The mature orchid soon bursts into bloom.

The plantlets are removed from the flask with tweezers, and the culture medium is rinsed off. The roots are then wrapped with sphagnum moss, and several plantlets are planted in a single pot *(right)*. Only when a plantlet has grown large enough to bear several bulbs at the base of its stem will it be transplanted to its own pot *(right, top)*.

Upon reaching a certain size, the globe is placed atop a gelatinous medium in another test tube *(above)*. The globe expands to cover the medium, and tiny plantlets emerge *(right)*.

The young plantlets are separated and transplanted onto a gelatinous medium in a flask *(near right)*. Four to six months later *(far right)*, the seedlings have grown firm roots and multiple leaves.

141

What Are Genetic Resources?

A wealth of genetic resources are helping plant breeders improve the quality, hardiness, and yield of modern crops. The three most useful resources are wild relatives of cultivated crops; land races, or crop strains that have been handed down from one generation of farmers to the next; and modern plant varieties that have been developed by botanists around the world.

In 1935, a Russian biologist and plant explorer named Nikolay Vavilov identified eight parts of the globe where most of today's cultivated crops originated. These crop centers correspond to areas of primitive agriculture, among them northern China, southwest Asia, southern Mexico, and Peru. Expanding on Vavilov's work, botanists have found that the greatest diversity of crop genetic resources occurs in areas where a continuous gene flow takes place between a crop under cultivation and its wild relatives growing in fields nearby.

Russian biologist Nikolay Vavilov championed the idea that crops and their wild relatives should be combined to produce higher-yielding and hardier plants. The first to clearly delineate crop origins, Vavilov identified eight geographical centers of plant genetic diversity.

Solanum demissum, the species of wild potato shown at left above, does not produce edible tubers, but it is nearly impervious to the potato disease known as late blight. Potato breeders therefore crossed *S. demissum* with the Kennebec potato *(right)* to produce a blight-resistant strain.

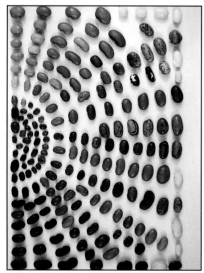

The type of bean cultivated by Indian farmers in Mexico and Central America often differed from one tribe to the next. Such variations in local diet preserved a broad base of genetic diversity for modern plant breeders.

The currant tomato *(above, left),* collected in Peru in 1929, was crossed with commercial tomato varieties in the early 1930s when growers discovered that the smaller fruit is immune to fusarium wilt. The disease-resistant by-product of this crossbreeding is shown at right.

Plant breeders prize genetic diversity because it enables them to create and maintain new varieties of crops. To safeguard this diversity, they use two methods. *In situ* conservation preserves wild species within their natural habitat, often in biological reserves. *Ex situ* conservation relies on the carefully controlled environment of a seed bank to ensure that the seeds of land races, genetic stocks, and obsolete cultivars will remain usable for decades. Vegetatively propagated plants are also conserved ex situ, but they require more delicate handling; they may be held in tissue-culture banks in a laboratory, or in a field gene bank that resembles an orchard.

The goal of all these measures is to preserve as much genetic variation of crop plants and their wild relatives as possible. No one can predict what crop disasters will occur in the future. Improving production methods will be the key to meeting the planet's food needs.

Because seeds are small and well adapted for storage, seed banks offer botanists a compact and convenient means for conserving crops and their wild relatives. Most crop seeds must be periodically grown into mature plants, from which new seeds are then collected for storage.

Plant physiologist Freddi Hammerschlag shows off a pair of disease-resistant peach-tree shoots grown by tissue culture. Hammerschlag grew each shoot from a single cell, after a two-year search in which she examined three million peach-tree cells. The two cells, both of which survived repeated exposure to leaf-spot toxin, matured into shoots in nutrient-filled glass jars.

A field gene bank in Brazil conserves a valuable stand of South American peach palms, whose recalcitrant seeds make the plants difficult to preserve in a seed bank. A field gene bank can be an arboretum, a botanical garden, a plantation, or any other land area in which a collection of growing plants is assembled and maintained.

Why Are Grains So Important?

Without the nutritious fruits of the grassy plants known as grains—especially corn, wheat, rice, barley, oats, and rye—much of the world's population would face starvation. Indeed, no other family of food plants feeds as many people as do the grasses.

Within the grass family, however, there is considerable variation from one edible plant to the next. Corn and rice differ most obviously from the other grains mentioned above. Significant differences also exist among wheat, barley, oats, and rye. These grains vary not only in character, size, shape, and hardiness, but in the extent of their cultivation and the uses to which they are put. This page takes a brief look at three of these vital crops.

The scoop on grains

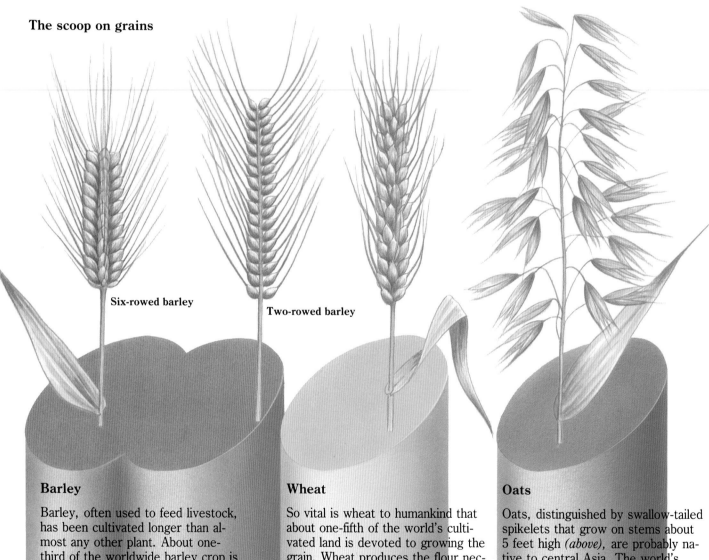

Six-rowed barley

Two-rowed barley

Barley

Barley, often used to feed livestock, has been cultivated longer than almost any other plant. About one-third of the worldwide barley crop is used to produce malt, an ingredient of beer. A hardy grain, barley grows as far north as the Arctic Circle and at high elevations in the Himalayas.

Wheat

So vital is wheat to humankind that about one-fifth of the world's cultivated land is devoted to growing the grain. Wheat produces the flour necessary for making bread and other baked goods as well as pasta. Although it originated in Asia, wheat is now cultivated all over the globe.

Oats

Oats, distinguished by swallow-tailed spikelets that grow on stems about 5 feet high *(above)*, are probably native to central Asia. The world's fourth most popular grain (behind wheat, rice, and corn), oats are the basis of oatmeal and many other food products for humans. They are also included in livestock fodder.

Glossary

Anther: The part of a stamen that makes and bears pollen.

Antheridium: The male reproductive organ in ferns, mosses, fungi, and algae.

Anthocyanin: A pigment that produces colors in the red, blue, and violet range.

Antipodal cell: One of three cells found in the embryo sac at the opposite end from the micropyle.

Archegonium: The female reproductive organ in ferns, mosses, fungi, and algae.

Arista: A bristlelike structure on the spikelets of grasses; also called an awn.

Ascocarp: The fruiting body of certain fungi, made up of a group of hyphae surrounding the asci.

Ascomycetes: Fungi that carry sexual spores in a sac, the ascus.

Asexual generation: The asexual, or sporophyte, generation in the alternation of generations.

Awn: A bristlelike projection found on the glumes of grasses.

Backcross: A plant-breeding technique in which a plant is crossed, or bred, with one of its parents.

Bacterium: A microscopic single-celled or noncelled organism often causing infection and disease.

Bract: A specialized leaf or leaflike part usually located at the base of a flower or inflorescence.

Callus: Regenerative cells that form when a plant is wounded.

Calyx: The green or leafy part of a flower consisting of sepals that help protect the developing reproductive parts of a flower.

Cambium: A layer of actively growing tissue. **Vascular cambium** lies between the xylem and phloem, producing new xylem cells on its inside and new phloem cells on its outside; **cork cambium** lies outside the vascular cambium and produces cork.

Carbohydrate: The main source of energy for most organisms, usually occurring in the form of sugars or starches.

Carotene: A yellow, orange, or red pigment.

Carotenoid: Any of a group of red and yellow pigments chemically similar to carotene and found in all photosynthesizing cells.

Carpel: A single seed-bearing organ of a flower, consisting of an ovary, a style, and a stigma.

Cellulose: A carbohydrate in plant cell walls that strengthens and hardens them.

Chlorophyll: A green pigment, found in all photosynthetic plants, that absorbs energy from sunlight to make food.

Chloroplast: The largest organelle in the cells of photosynthetic plants; it contains chlorophyll.

Chromosome: The carrier of genes within the nucleus of a cell.

Conjugation: A form of sexual reproduction in which a male gamete fuses with a female gamete to form a zygote.

Cork: A layer of protective tissue that replaces the epidermis in trees. Dead cork cells form the bark.

Corm: A swollen underground stem similar to a bulb.

Corolla: The petals of a flower. The corolla lies inside the calyx and helps protect the developing reproductive parts.

Cortex: The layer of tissue that lies between the epidermis and the vascular tissue.

Crossbreeding: The breeding of two individuals of different species or varieties in order to produce a hybrid.

Cross-fertilization: The fertilization of an ovule by the sperm from a different individual of the same species.

Culm: A jointed stem, usually found in grasses and sedges.

Cupule: A cup-shaped outgrowth in mosses and liverworts that contains the gemmae.

Deciduous: Shedding the leaves annually.

Diploid (2n): Having two sets of chromosomes.

Drupe: Any fruit developed from a single ovary, with an outer skin, a pulpy middle layer, and a hard shell around the seed.

Embryo: The young plant usually contained in a seed.

Endosperm: The storage tissue in the seeds of most angiosperms that provides food for the embryo.

Enzyme: A protein that triggers and speeds up chemical reactions within cells.

Filament: The stalklike part of the stamen, bearing the anther at its tip.

Fructose: A sugar found in fruits.

Fucoxanthin: A carotenoid pigment in seaweed.

Funicle: The stalk attaching the ovule, and later the seed, to the ovary wall.

Gall: An abnormal swelling on plants caused by insects, or a sterile female flower found on some plants, such as figs.

Gamete: A mature sexual reproductive cell, either a sperm or an egg, that unites with another cell to form a zygote.

Gametophyte: The generation in an alternation of generations that produces gametes.

Gemma: A unit of vegetative reproduction in mosses and liverworts, that when separated from the parent develops into a new plant. Plural: **gemmae.**

Gene: A distinct unit of hereditary material.

Germ cell: A sexual reproductive cell.

Glucose: A basic sugar found in most plant tissues that is used to make starch, cellulose, sucrose, and other carbohydrates.

Glume: One of a pair of bracts beneath the inflorescence of grasses and sedges.

Gonidium: Any of the algal cells in a lichen.

Granum: One of the structural units of a chloroplast.

Gymnosperm: A plant that bears "naked" seeds, or seeds that are not enclosed in an ovary.

Haploid (n): Having one set of chromosomes.

Herbaceous: Pertaining to plants that do not have woody stems.

Heteromorphism: A life cycle in which the alternating generations are distinctly different in size and shape.

Hormone: A substance, such as auxin, found in plants that controls the growth of plant tissue.

Hybrid: An individual plant produced by parents of different species or varieties.

Hymenium: A fertile layer consisting of asci that lines the ascocarp of a fungus or the gills of a mushroom.

Hypha: One of the threadlike, branched filaments that make up a fungal mycelium. Plural: **hyphae.**

Hypocotyl: The part of a plant embryo that connects the seed leaves to the radicle and develops into the end of the stem.

Inbreeding: Reproduction using the ovule and sperm from the same or closely related individuals.

Indusium: A flap of tissue that covers each cluster of spore cases on a fern.

Inflorescence: A cluster of flowers arranged on a single axis.

Integument: A protective skin or rind that develops from the base of an ovule and encloses it almost entirely.

Inulin: A type of fructose stored in the roots of certain plants.

Isomorphism: A life cycle in which the alternating generations are identical.

Lamina: The flattened, bladelike portion of a leaf.

Laminarin: A glucose in algae formed by photosynthesis.

Land race: A primitive variety of a plant that originated and persisted in cultivation.

Lemma: The lower of a pair of bracts below each flower in a grass inflorescence.

Mannitol: A common sugar alcohol in lichens and fungi.

Meristem: The growth tissue of plants, made up of actively dividing cells. **Apical meristem** is the growth tissue at the tip of a stem; **ground meristem** produces the pith and the cortex.

Mesophyll: Tissue that forms the interior parts of a leaf.

Mold: A fungus that produces a distinct mycelium, often in the form of a furry coating, on dead or decaying matter.

Motor cell: A cell that conveys an impulse that results in motion.

Mutation: A random, inheritable change in the genetic pattern of an organism.

Mycelium: A mass of branching hyphae that forms the body of most fungi. Plural: **mycelia.**

Myxamoeba: A swarm cell that has lost its tail.

Nucellus: The rounded mass of tissue in an ovule that contains the embryo sac; it is surrounded by the integument.

Organelle: A specialized structure within a cell designed to perform a function, such as respiration or cell defense.

Ovary: The swollen lower part of the carpel containing the ovules. After fertilization, the ovary forms the fruit.

Ovule: The plant part that contains the embryo sac and the ovum and that after fertilization develops into a seed.

Ovum: The female reproductive cell.

Palea: The upper of a pair of bracts below each flower in the grass inflorescence.

Parasite: An organism that obtains food or shelter at the expense of another organism, called the host.

Perennial: A plant with a life cycle that lasts several years.

Pericarp: The walls of a plant ovary.

Perithecium: The globular or flask-shaped body that encloses the asci in some fungi.

Petal: One of the floral leaves that form the corolla. Petals are often fragrant and brightly colored to attract pollinators.

Phloem: The vascular tissue that transports food from the leaves to the stem and roots. The phloem is made up of sieve tubes and other tissues and occurs with the xylem.

Pistil: The ovule-bearing organ of a seed plant.

Pith: The spongy cylinder of tissue in the center of the stem.

Plumule: The bud of an embryo that forms the stem and leaves.

Pollen: Fine, powdery grains containing male reproductive cells.

Pollination: Transfer of pollen from the anther to the stigma.

Polyploid: Having more than two sets of chromosomes.

Progenitor: A biologically related ancestor, particularly the originator of a certain line of development.

Prothallium: The gametophyte of ferns and related plants.

Protoembryo: The earliest form of an embryo.

Radicle: The lower part of the embryo that forms the root.

Resin: A substance in certain vascular plants that hardens when exposed to air.

Respiration: The process in which a cell takes in oxygen for energy and releases carbon dioxide and water.

Rhizoid: One of the rootlike threads in mosses, ferns, and liverworts that anchor the plant and absorb water and nutrients.

Rhizome: A rootlike underground stem that grows horizontally.

Sap: The mixture of water, sugars, and minerals in plants.

Scale: A specialized leaf that encloses an immature leaf bud.

Scion: A shoot, twig, or bud taken from one plant and joined by grafting to another plant.

Sepal: One of the floral leaves that lie outside the petals of a flower and protect the reproductive organs as they develop.

Sexual generation: The sexual, or gametophyte, generation in the alternation of generations.

Sieve tube: A continuous series of cells in the phloem, forming a tube to conduct food.

Slime mold: A type of fungus made up of a mobile jellylike mass that reproduces by spores.

Soredium: A group of algal cells surrounded by fungal hyphae that acts as an agent of vegetative reproduction in lichens. Plural: **soredia.**

Sperm: A male reproductive cell.

Spike: An inflorescence in which the flowers are borne directly on a long stalk.

Spore: A simple asexual unit of reproduction capable of forming a new individual directly.

Sporophore: A fungus hypha specialized to bear spores.

Sporophyll: A modified leaf that bears a plant's spore cases.

Sporophyte: The generation in the alternation of generations that produces spores.

Stamen: The pollen-bearing organ of a flower, consisting of the filament and the anther.

Starch: A carbohydrate made up of sugars or made by plants through photosynthesis.

Stele: The central core of roots and stems of vascular plants, consisting of the vascular tissue, the pith, and the pericycle.

Stem: The part of the plant axis that is usually above ground and bears the leaves, the reproductive parts, and the buds.

Stigma: The part of a pistil that receives the pollen.

Stipule: One of a pair of leaflike or scaly structures at the base of a leaf that protects the leaf as it develops.

Stock: A plant onto which the scion of another plant is grafted.

Stoma: A small pore in the epidermis through which gases are exchanged in photosynthesis, respiration, and transpiration.

Stroma: The supporting framework of a chloroplast, containing the chemicals needed for certain photosynthetic reactions.

Style: The stalklike structure between the ovary and the stigma.

Succulent: A plant adapted to live through periods of drought by storing water in swollen leaves and stems.

Sucrose: A simple carbohydrate and the major plant sugar.

Swarm cell: An amoeba-like cell in slime mold that moves by means of a tail.

Symbiosis: A usually beneficial relationship between two organisms that live together.

Synergid: One of two haploid nuclei of unknown function near the micropyle in the embryo sac.

Thylakoid: A sac lined with a membrane containing chlorophyll in the grana of chloroplasts, where photosynthesis takes place.

Tissue: Cells that form the structural materials of plants.

Transpiration: The passage of water vapor through a plant from the roots through the vascular system to the atmosphere.

Vacuole: A cavity in a cell that stores food and other minerals.

Vascular: Provided with ducts or tissues, for conducting fluids.

Vegetative reproduction: A form of asexual reproduction in which parts of the parent plant detach and form new individuals.

Xylem: Tissue made of vessels and woody fibers that provides support and conducts water and nutrients upward from the roots.

Zoospore: An asexual spore produced by certain algae and fungi, capable of moving by means of a tail.

Zygospore: A thick-walled zygote formed by the fusion of two similar gametes in conjugation.

Zygote: The cell produced by the fusion of a male and a female gamete before it divides, or the fertilized egg.

Index

E

Earthstar (mushroom), *99*
Edelweiss, *121*
Egg, fertilized, *9*
Elaeagnus, thorny, *29*
Elder, red-berry, bark of, *27*
Elodea nuttalli (water plant), *129*
Embryo, *12;* development of, *9*
Embryo culture, *140*
Endodermis of root, *15*
Endoplasmic reticulum, *6, 7*
Endosperm, *8-9, 12,* 66; coconut, *86-87*
Epidermis, *20;* of cactus, *113;* of pine
    needles, *49;* prickles as outgrowths
    of, *28;* of root, *15;* stomas in, *39*
Epiphytes (air plants), *22-23*
Eucalyptus trees, *118-119;* giant, *122*
Eumycetes vs. Myxomycetes, *96*
Evening primrose, *53*
Evergreens: defoliation, *43;* and ice ag-
    es, *120-121;* mistletoe, *23, 82-83;*
    oak, fruit of, *77. See also* Conifers

F

False acacia tree, *28*
Fenestraria (window-leaf plant), *115*
Ferns, *95, 108-109*
Fertilization, *8,* 66; in algae, *103;* in
    ferns and mosses, *109*
Fescue, red, *63*
Ficus tree, buttress roots of, *23*
Figs and fig wasps, *67, 68-69*
Figwort, *57*
Fir, Douglas, *122*
Firethorn, *78*
Fleming, Sir Alexander, *132*
Floral regions of Earth, *map* 118-119
Florey, Howard, 132
Flowers and flowering plants, 50-63;
    alpine zone, *120, 121;* biggest (*Raffle-
    sia arnoldii*), *51, 56-57;* day length
    and blooming of, *54-55;* vs. gymno-
    sperms, 8, 88; in vitro cultivation of,
    140-141; male and female parts, 51,
    52-53, 58-59, 62; medicines from,
    132; opening and closing of, *60-61;*
    parasites, *23, 51, 56-57, 82-83;* polli-
    nation, *8, 50, 52-53,* 56, 58, 59, 62,
    68, 69, 84, 85, 95, 136-137; sexes,
    separate, *58-59,* 68, 69, *83, 84-85;*
    structure of, *52-53;* tetraploid, *139;*
    vegetative reproduction, *62, 90-91,
    134-135, 140-141, 143. See also* Crop
    plants; Fruits; Seeds; *and individual
    names*
Food chain, *124-125*
Fruits, *8, 64-65;* baobab, *117;* coconuts,
    86-87; coloration of, *78-79;* corn, *84-
    85;* cucumbers, *30,* 77; figs, *67, 68-
    69;* flowers' making of, *66-67, 68-69;*
    popping open of, *76-77;* simple vs.
    complex, *66-67;* squash, *58. See also*
    Crop plants; Seeds
Fungi, *96-97;* as decomposers, *126;* in
    lichens, *106, 107;* mushrooms, *92-93,
    95, 98-99, 126;* as penicillin source,
    132-133

G

Gametophytes. *See* Spore-bearing plants
Gamma field, *138-139*
Gene bank, field, *143*
General Sherman (sequoia), 122
Genetic resources and genetic diversity,
    131, *142-143*
Genetics and plant breeding, 136, *138-
    139*
Gentians, opening and closing of, *61*
Geotropism, *15*
Germination, *8, 12-13, 79,* 80, *81, 88,
    95;* algae, *102;* mosses, *109*
Glaciation and tundra plants, *120-121*
Gladiolus, *91*
Golgi apparatus, *6, 7*
Gourds: grafting onto, *135;* leaf growth
    in, *17;* root pressure in, *21*
Grafting, *134-135*
Grains, *144;* corn as, *84-85, 136-137;*
    rice, *67, 139;* wheat, *55, 67, 144*
Grana in chloroplasts, *10-11*
Grapes, *67;* tendrils on plants, *29,* 30
Grasses: bamboo, *32-33, 91;* flowers,
    62-63; Oplismenus, 75; pampas, Japa-
    nese, *73. See also* Grains
Green algae, *105*
Green bean seed, germination of, *12-13*
Gromwell, callus culture of, *140*
Growth rings, tree trunk's, *18-19, 24-25*
Guard cells, stomas', *39*
Gum (eucalyptus) trees, *118-119,* 122
Gymnosperms: vs. angiosperms, 8, 88;
    cycads, *59. See also* Conifers

H

Hammerschlag, Freddi, *143*
Haptonasty, 44, *45*
Haustoria (parasitic roots), *23, 57, 83*
Heartwood, formation of, 24
Hermaphroditic plants, techniques of, *59*
Heterosis (hybrid vigor), 136, 137
Himalayan cedar cone, *89*
Homology and analogy, *29*
Horsetails, *94, 95*
Hybrid plants, *136-137, 142*

Hypocotyl, *12-13*

I

Ice ages and tundra plants, *120-121*
Inarching, *135*
Inbreeding of corn, *136-137*
Inflorescences: dandelion, *72;* fig vs.
    pineapple, *69;* sunflower, *70, 71;* this-
    tle, *74*
Insectivorous plants, *34-35, 46-47*
Insects: fungi living off, *97;* orchid re-
    sembling, *53;* pollination by, *8, 50,
    52-53,* 56, 68, 69; as primary consum-
    ers, *125;* seeds spread by, *79;* soil
    animals, *127;* trapped by plants, *34-
    35, 46-47, 53*
In situ vs. *ex situ* conservation, *142-143*
Inulin grain, *7*
In vitro cultivation, *140-141, 143*
Iris, *55;* fruit of, *67*
Ivy, roots of, for support, *23, 29*

J

Japanese pampas grass, *73*
Jew's ear (mushroom), *98*

K

Kandelia mangrove seedlings, *80*
Kapok tree, *123*
Kauri pine, *123*
Kelp, life cycle of, *103*
Kudzu vine, *75*

L

Land races, beans as, *142*
Larch trees, *119;* cone, *89;* trunk, *24-25*
Lateral roots, 14, *15*
Lawn grass, *62-63*
Leaves, 34-49; arrangement of, *36-37;*
    bamboo sheaths, *32, 33;* blooming
    triggered by, *54-55;* cactus, primitive,
    113; cells, *4-5;* color changes, *40-41;*
    eucalyptus, *118;* fallen, decay of, *126-
    127;* falling, cause of, *41, 42-43;* ferns
    vs. mosses, 108; growth of, 16, *17;*
    of insect-eating plants, *34-35, 46-47;*
    mimosa, curling of, *44-45;* modifica-
    tions of, *28, 29, 30;* mutant, *139;* new
    plants grown on, *90-91;* palm tree,
    86-87; photosynthesis in, 6, *10-11,
    38;* pine needles, *43, 48-49;* rosette
    of, *8;* seasonal changes, *34-35, 40-41,
    42-43, 126;* seed leaves (cotyledons),
    development of, *9, 12, 13, 79,* 88;
    shape of, *37;* stomas, *20, 21, 38-39,
    40, 49;* of stone plant, *110, 114-115;*
    water transportation to, *20-21, 40-41*

modifications of, *29;* water transportation from, *20, 21, 40-41*
Roses, *28-29*
Rowan seeds, spreading of, *78-79*
Runners, reproduction by, *91*
Ryegrass, Italian, *63*

S

Saguaro cactus, *111, 113*
Salvia flower, *53*
Saprophytes, defined, 57, 96
Saprophytic chain, defined, 126
Sarracenia pitcher plant, *47*
Sea fan, *105*
Sea lettuce, *102-103;* spores, *95, 102*
Seaweed, *95, 102-103, 104-105*
Sedum, *90-91;* stomas, *38*
Seeds, 64-65; animals' spreading of, 65, 74, 75, 77, *78-79, 82;* dandelion, *67, 72-73;* development of, on tree, *80-81;* germination of, *8, 12-13, 79,* 80, *81, 88, 95;* making of, *8-9,* 66; mistletoe, spreading of, *82-83;* nuts, 65, *77;* in pine cones, *88-89;* polyploidic breeding, *138-139;* from popping fruits, *76-77; Rafflesia,* 56; simple vs. complex fruits, *66, 67;* vs. spores, *94-95;* with sticking properties, *74-75;* storage of, *143;* sunflower, *70;* windborne, *72-73, 88*
Sequoias, *122-123*
Sexes of flowers, separate, *58-59;* corn, *84-85;* fig, 68, 69; mistletoe, *83*
Shepherd's-purse, *8, 67*
Shield lichen, *107*
Shiitake mushrooms, *95;* spores, *99*
Shoots: bamboo, *32-33, 91;* growth of, *16*
Shoot-tip culture, *140-141*
Slime molds, 96, *97*
Soil animals, *110-111, 127*
Solidago, *73*
Sorrel, wood: *77;* photonasty in, *45*
Sow thistle, *73*
Soybeans, *13, 54, 67*
Sperm, fertilization by, *8,* 66; in algae, *103;* in ferns and mosses, *109*
Spiderwort stoma, *38*
Spikelets, grass, *62;* on oats, *144*
Spinach, *136;* as long-day plant, 54
Spindle tree, *78*
Spines, *28;* of cacti, *112, 113*
Sponge gourds: leaf growth, *17;* root pressure, *21*
Spongy tissue, *39, 40, 41*
Spore-bearing plants, 92-109; ascocarps (fruiting bodies), *97, 106;* in evolution,

93, 94; ferns, *95, 108-109;* molds as, *96-97;* mosses as, *95, 108-109;* mushrooms as, *95, 99;* seaweed as, *95, 102-103;* vs. seed plants, *94-95*
Sporophytes. *See* Spore-bearing plants
Squash, male and female flowers of, *58-59*
Squirting cucumber, *77*
Stamens, 51, *52-53, 58, 59, 62*
Starch grains, *7, 11*
Stele, *15*
Stems, 19; bamboo, *32-33;* bark on, trees', *25, 26-27;* big tree trunks, *116, 117, 122-123;* cacti, 112, *113;* ferns vs. mosses, 108; growth of, *16, 17;* growth rings, trees', *18-19, 24-25;* hypocotyl, *12-13;* layers of, *20;* leaf arrangement on, *36-37;* modifications of, *28, 29, 30-31;* of parasite and host, 57; receptacle tissue in fruits, *67, 68, 69;* runners, *91;* underground, reproduction by, *62, 91;* water transportation through, *20-21, 40-41*
Stomas, *20, 21, 38-39, 40;* cactus, *113;* pine needles, *49*
Stonecrop (sedum), *90-91;* stomas, *38*
Stone plants, *110, 114-115*
Storage grains, *7, 11*
Strawberries: anther culture, *140;* fruit, *67;* plants with runners, *91*
Streptomyces antibiotics, 132, 133
Succession of plants, *128-129*
Sundew, *34-35, 47*
Sunflowers, *70-71;* phyllotaxis, *36-37*
Sunlight. *See* Light
Swallowtail butterflies, *50, 53*
Sweet pea, *55*
Sweet potato, *29;* grafting onto, *135*
Sycamore tree, *26-27*

T

Taenophyllum root, *29*
Tendrils, *29;* cucumber, coiling of, *30-31*
Test-tube cultivation, *140-141, 143*
Tetraploid plants, *139*
Thallus lichens, *107*
Thistles, *74*
Thorns, 28; parts analogous to, *28, 29*
Thylakoids, *10-11*
Tickseed fruit, *75*
Timberline, 120
Tissue culture, *140-141, 143*
Toadstools, *92-93, 98-99*
Tomatoes, crossbred, *136, 142*
Touch, mimosa's response to, 44, *45*
Touch-me-not, *76, 77*
Transpiration, *20, 21*

Trees: acacia, false, *28;* baobab, *116-117;* bark, *25, 26-27;* bottle tree, *117;* chestnut, parts of, *43, 59, 67, 77;* with colorful fruits, *78-79;* eucalyptus, *118-119, 122;* grafting, *134-135;* growth rings, *18-19, 24-25;* ice ages and, *120-121;* larches, *119;* largest, *122-123;* lichens on, *107;* mangrove, *80-81;* needles, *43, 48-49;* oldest, *123;* palm, *86-87, 143;* parasites on, *23, 82-83;* roots, *18-19, 22, 23, 29;* seasonal changes, *34-35, 40-41, 42-43, 126;* seeds, *67, 73, 77, 79, 88-89,* 94; sequoias, *122-123;* succession of, *128;* water transportation through, *20-21, 40-41*
Tubers, *91*
Tulips: bulbs, *60-61, 91*
Tundra plants, ice ages and, *120-121*

V

Vacuoles, *6, 7*
Vascular bundles, *20, 49, 113*
Vavilov, Nikolai, *142*
Vegetative reproduction, *90-91;* grafting, *134-135;* tissue culture, *140-141, 143;* underground stems, *62, 91*
Venus's-flytrap, *46*
Vines: ivy, roots of, *23, 29;* kudzu, *75; Nepenthes, 47;* tendrils, *29, 30-31*
Violets: fruit and seeds, *67, 77, 79;* self-pollinating, *69*

W

Waksman, Selman, 132
Wasps, fig, pollination by, 68, *69*
Water lilies, *119, 129*
Watermelons: grafting, *135;* seedless, *139*
Water plants, *129;* diatoms, *100-101;* roots of, *23;* seaweed, *95, 102-103, 104-105;* water lilies, *119, 129*
Water potential, 20, 21
Waxwings, Bohemian, fruit eaten by, *78-79*
Wegener, Alfred, 119
Wheat, *55, 67, 144*
White pine, *49*
Window-leaf plant, *115*
Wood sorrel, *77;* photonasty in, *45*

X

Xylem: in roots, *14, 15;* in stems and trunks, *19, 20, 24-25, 26, 27*

Z

Zelkova, bark of, *27*

Staff for
UNDERSTANDING SCIENCE & NATURE

Assistant Managing Editor: Patricia Daniels
Editorial Directors: Allan Fallow, Karin Kinney
Assistant Editor/Research: Elizabeth Thompson
Editorial Assistant: Marike van der Veen
Production Manager: Marlene Zack
Senior Copyeditors: Juli Duncan, Anne Farr
Copyeditor: Donna Carey
Picture Coordinator: David A. Herod
Production: Celia Beattie
Library: Louise D. Forstall
Computer Composition: Deborah G. Tait (Manager), Monika D.
    Thayer, Janet Barnes Syring, Lillian Daniels

Special Contributors, Text: Joe Alper, John Clausen, Marfé
    Ferguson Delano, Mark Galan, Stephen Hart, Barbara Mallen
Research: Eugenia Scharf, Lauren V. Scharf
Design/Illustration: Antonio Alcalá, Nicholas Fasciano,
    David Neal Wiseman
Photography: Cover: © Perry D. Slocum, A.P.S.A. 1: Sean Morris,
    Oxford Scientific Films, Long Hanborough, Oxfordshire, England.
    123: © Whit Bronaugh. 130, 131: Art by Al Kettler. 142: Art by
    Al Kettler, photo USDA, courtesy John L. Creech. 143: Art by
    Al Kettler, photo courtesy Agricultural Research Service, USDA.
    144: Art by Al Kettler (chicken and bowl).
Index: Barbara L. Klein

Consultant:
    Dr. John L. Creech, former director of the U.S. National Arbore-
    tum, is recognized as one of the leading plant explorers of this
    century in the United States.

Library of Congress Cataloging-in-Publication Data
Plant life.
        p.   cm. — (Understanding science & nature)
    Includes index.
    Summary: Uses a question and answer format to discuss the
structure and function of plants.
    ISBN 0-8094-9712-3 (trade) — ISBN 0-8094-9713-1 (lib. bdg.)
    1. Plants—Miscellanea—Juvenile literature.
2. Botany—Miscellanea—Juvenile literature.
[1. Plants—Miscellanea. 2. Botany—Miscellanea.
3. Questions and answers.]
I. Time-Life Books. II. Series.
QK49.P515 1993
581—dc20   92-34975
                                              CIP
                                               AC

TIME-LIFE for CHILDREN ®

President: Robert H. Smith
Associate Publisher and Managing Editor: Neil Kagan
Assistant Managing Editors: Patricia Daniels, Elizabeth Ward
Editorial Directors: Jean Burke Crawford, Allan Fallow,
    Karin Kinney, Sara Mark
Director of Marketing: Margaret Mooney
Product Managers: Cassandra Ford, Amy Haworth,
    Shelley L. Schimkus
Director of Finance: Lisa Peterson
Administrative Assistant: Barbara A. Jones

Original English translation by International Editorial Services Inc./
C. E. Berry

First printing. Printed in U.S.A.
Published simultaneously in Canada.
Time Life Inc. is a wholly owned subsidiary of
THE TIME INC. BOOK COMPANY.
TIME-LIFE is a trademark of Time Warner Inc. U.S.A.
For subscription information, call 1-800-621-7026.